MADAME MILLENNIAL

MADAME MILLENNIAL

100 Tips to Help the Modern Woman Master Work, Life, and Everything In Between

Kelli Clifton Ogunsanya

Copyright © 2017 — Kelli Clifton Ogunsanya

ALL RIGHTS RESERVED—No part of this book may be reproduced in any form or by any electronic or mechanical means, including information storage and retrieval systems, without permission in writing from the authors, except by a reviewer who may quote brief passages in a review.

Published by Deeds Publishing in Athens, GA
www.deedspublishing.com

Printed in The United States of America

Cover design by Ashley Clarke

Library of Congress Cataloging-in-Publications data is available upon request.

ISBN 978-1-947309-00-5

Books are available in quantity for promotional or premium use. For information, email info@deedspublishing.com.

First Edition, 2017

10 9 8 7 6 5 4 3 2 1

It is no secret that endless misconceptions exist about millennials. From how we approach the traditional workplace environment, to habits about saving money, or even our desire to have a career driven by purpose over profit, we can be challenging to characterize and seldom fit into a single mold. Regardless of the perception, one undoubtable trait of millennials is our propensity to become unique trailblazers, setting our own cadence for navigating and succeeding in today's society.

Within the broader millennial population, there is one demographic that stands out from the rest due to their endless ambition, glass-ceiling-shattering successes, and uncanny determination to lead personally and professionally fulfilling lives. That group is none other than millennial women.

Women in general are multi-faceted, dynamic individuals who spend much of their time playing the role of caregiver, coach, mentor, and champion to others while sacrificing their own personal and professional successes.

For some women, juggling all aspects of their life is no major feat. For others, the task can be daunting and downright overwhelming. To make matters more challenging, today's age of social media, instant gratification, and fast-paced society, makes it all too easy to get caught up in life's rat race and unrealistically compare our worth and purpose to other women.

Constant comparisons to other women often raise an age-old question: "Can we have it all?" The simple truth is that while some women may "have it all," they seldom have it at the same time!

In pursuit of this question, millennial women, born in the early 1980s through mid-1990s, are in a unique situation. Over half of us were born to Baby Boomers, whose outlook on career progression, family planning, and financial management is viewed by some millennials as risk-adverse and conservative. This perspective, combined with many millennial's desires to pursue entrepreneurship early in their careers, to seek job opportunities that prioritize passion and purpose, and to delay marriage or child-rearing until our later years, has changed the way these we approach the workplace and define personal success and satisfaction.

In terms of the workplace, millennial women are in an unprecedented situation. For many millennials, it is not uncommon to work with or even manage co-workers spanning multi-generations (Generation X, Generation Y, and Baby Boomers). This requires us to be savvy, deliberate, and to understand the "rules of engagement" for long-standing success and professional development.

For many women, professional and personal success is achieved through having a strong network of mentors and confidants invested in their wellbeing and development. It is through this network and sharing of valuable lessons that women excel both in and out of the workplace.

Inspired by the countless conversations I have had with young women over the years, this book is meant to offer fellow millennial women a snapshot of select life lessons, insights, guidance, and tips for mastering whatever stage of life you are in, whether at work or as a wife, mother, sister, daughter, or friend.

To help guide your reading experience, I've included a visual

"Life Wheel," which represents key aspects of one's life (Health, Finances, Work etc.). Additionally, each chapter of this book also aligns with one of these categories, offering you the opportunity to focus your reading on specific areas. Prior to reading the chapters, take a moment to rate (0 lowest, 9 highest) your current personal satisfaction with each area of the wheel. Consider spending more time in chapters focused on areas you've rated 6 or below to ensure you are living your best life.

Madame Millennial: Life Wheel

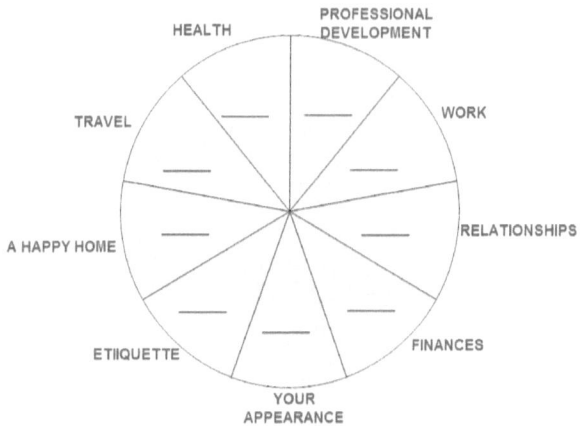

Some chapters, such as "How to Build Your Brand," "How to Be a Great Party Host," or "Top Financial Mistakes Millennial Women Make," may contain information that you already understand and live by. However, old truths die hard and revisiting these topics can never hurt.

Your time is valuable. As such, each chapter was written to be a quick read packed with information that you can consume now and use later.

My hope is that this book will be a lifelong personal growth guide that not only helps you navigate different phases of your life, but also serves as a resource that you can share with another millennial woman or a loved one.

Cheers to you… Madame Millennial!

Kelli

Contents

1. YOUR HEALTH   1
   Managing Stress   2
   How To Get Out Of A Rut   3
   5 Things Smart Women Do to De-Stress   5
   Maturity, Is That You? How To Recognize You Are Changing For The Better   8
   Key Healthcare Numbers to Know   10
   Understanding Your Health Insurance   11
   What to Do When Your Medical Information is Incorrect   13
   Finding a New Medical Provider   14
   10 Health Symptoms You Should Not Ignore   15
   10 Personal Documents to Have Readily Accessible   16
   Skin Care 101   17

2. PROFESSIONAL DEVELOPMENT   19
   Building Your Brand   20
   How to Become a Valuable Employee   22
   5 Ways Entry Level Millennial Employees Sabotage Career Progress   24
   How to Get Introduced to Someone You Professionally Admire   25
   Navigating a Room When You Know No One   27
   3 Ways to Stop Getting Interrupted When You Speak   28
   Commanding Respect in a Multi-Generational Workforce: 3 Things Millennial Women Must Know   30
   The Value of the Informational Interview   32
   Asking for a Letter of Recommendation   35
   The Art of the Follow-Up   37
   Business Cards   39
   How to Join a Board   40
   8 Ways to Be a Successful College Applicant   41

3. WORK 45

Resume 101 47

Top Interview Tips 49

Navigating the Interview Process 51

Responding to Job Offers 53

Non-Compete Agreements 101 56

Mastering the First 30 Days of a New Job 58

How to Find a Mentor and Sponsor 60

How to Ask for a Raise 62

How to Take a Vacation and Not Feel Overwhelmed When You Return 64

How to Upward Manage Your Boss 66

Handling Workplace Discrimination and Harassment 67

4 Steps to Take After Not Getting Promoted 70

Managing an Unfulfilling Job 72

Being Laid Off from a Job 75

The Art of Delegation and Why You Need to Do It Now 77

Resigning from a Job 80

4. RELATIONSHIPS 83

How to Be a Great Friend 84

When Your Friendship Circles Clash 87

7 Tough Conversations to Have with Yourself Each Year 89

Outgrowing Friends 90

Cohabitation with a Significant Other 91

Making a Great First Impression 93

10 Reasons You Should Think Twice Before Marriage 94

How to Be a Great Bridesmaid 95

How to Be a Great Party Host 97

5 Easy Ways to Perform

Random Acts of Kindness 99

5. FINANCES 101

Top Financial Mistakes Millennial Women Make 102

10 Financial Tools that Every Millennial Woman Needs	103
What Is an Emergency Fund?	104
Why Financial Autonomy is Critical for Millennial Women	105
Monitoring Your Credit	106
How to Start Investing with Any Income Amount	108
How to Pay Down Debt	110
Handling a Declined Card	111
Maximizing Your Earning Potential	112
Pre-Nup or Nope?	113
Staying in Control of Your Money	115
5 Reasons to Start Advanced Planning Now	118
Financial Tips for College Bound Millennials	121
Champagne Life on a Beer Budget	123

6. YOUR APPEARANCE — 125

The Value of Self-Awareness	126
5 Quick Tips to Make a Lasting First Impression	128
Clothing Essentials	129
Capsule Wardrobe	131
Clothing Terminology 101	133
Essential Jewelry 101	136
Hair Care 101	138
10 Things to Always Have in Your Purse	141
Handling Clothing Mishaps with Ease	142

7. MADAME MILLENNIAL ETIQUETTE — 145

10 Commandments of Work Place Communication	147
10 Ways You Are Unknowingly Offensive	149
How to Start (and Hold) Great Conversations	150
Responding to a Question When You Do Not Know the Answer	151
The Importance of Timeliness	152
The Rules for RSVP-ing	154

Email 101	156
Telephone 101	158
Stationery	161
Headphone Etiquette	162
Mastering Unspoken Communication	163
Alcohol Dos and Don'ts	165
20 Restaurant Words to Master	167
8. A BALANCED HOME	**169**
Gaining Efficiency in Your Life	171
Ten Ways to Save Time During Your Day	173
Maximizing Your Grocery Shopping Experience	174
Kitchen Must-Haves	176
Fail-Proof Recipes	178
Fail-proof Home Cleaning Tips	187
Spring Cleaning	189
Bathroom Cabinet Essentials	193
Junk Drawer Judy	195
How Often Do I? Rules of the Home	196
9. TRAVEL	**199**
Packing Rules for Long or Short Term Travel	200
Travel Tips for Millennial Women	203
Disruptions in Travel Plans	206
Handling a Minor Car Accident	208
5 Ways to Save Money When Traveling	209
About the Author	**211**

1. Your Health

Health is the topic of the first chapter due to the overwhelming importance of mental, physical, and spiritual wellbeing. As much as we may aim to be superwomen, if our health is not in order, nothing is in order. It is imperative that you prioritize your personal well-being in order to excel personally and professionally.

This chapter covers the following:

- Managing Stress
- How to Get Out of a Rut
- 5 Things Smart Women Do to De-stress
- Maturity, Is that You? How to Recognize When You Are Changing for the Better
- Key Healthcare Numbers to Know
- Understand Your Health Insurance
- What to Do When Your Medical Information Is Incorrect
- Finding a New Medical Provider
- 10 Health Symptoms You Should Not Ignore
- 10 Personal Documents to Have Readily Accessible
- Skin Care 101

Managing Stress

Have you ever had moments when everything seems to be going wrong? Your rent is past due, you messed up the presentation at work (again), your relationship with your significant other is off-track, your skin is off-balanced, your hair seems thinner for no reason, and you cannot remember the last time you had a good night's sleep.

Stress at home, work, and in your personal life can take a silent but noticeable toll on your overall well-being. Too often, women juggle a million things at once while masking stress under the veil of being a superwoman. Without question, stress can have emotional and physical ramifications ranging from depression to high blood pressure or a heart attack.

Here are a few tips on keeping stress manageable:

- Learn to say no to tasks and requests that add no additional value to your life
- Stop apologizing for putting yourself first
- Develop a daily routine such as meditation, prayer, tea time, journaling, or exercise
- Manage your time with to-do lists
- Outsource errands by shopping online for groceries, using home delivery services, & using auto bill-pay for financial management
- Practice clean eating by consuming unprocessed foods and limiting sugar intake
- Prepare and freeze meals on the weekends for consumption during the work week

How To Get Out Of A Rut

Do you ever find yourself frustrated, depressed, or confused, wanting a change but unsure how to go about it? Whether it is in our personal life, profession, or relationship with a significant other, we all get in ruts, deserving better for ourselves but lacking a clear path forward.

The next time you face such a situation, consider the following recommendations to help you gain clarity and develop a plan of action.

Acknowledge that you are stuck

Although seemingly simple, the first step is to recognize and verbalize that something in your life needs to change.

Visualize what you want

If your goal is to lose 20 pounds or to find a new job, define your goal and give yourself a timeline. Common tools such as app-based trackers, vision boards, or daily journals help you visualize and meet your goals.

Have an accountability partner

A support system is critical to reaching and maintaining your goal. Whether it be a workout buddy, coworker, or mentor, it is important that you have someone cheering in your corner and encouraging you to move forward.

Break down your goal into small but meaningful steps

Change can be overwhelming if you try to accomplish everything at once. Segmenting your goals allows you to accomplish small wins and stay motivated. As you hit your milestones, don't forget to celebrate and realize how far you have come.

Be patient with yourself

Too often we focus on the end goal rather than enjoying our growth. As you continue to progress, it is not uncommon to fall off track or suffer from burn-out. Allow yourself time to re-focus, resume tracking your progress, and reach your goal on your own terms.

5 Things Smart Women Do to De-Stress

Throughout life, you will always encounter some level of stress and chaos. Consistent stress often jeopardizes your daily routine and results in ineffective time management and feeling as though you have no control. To keep stress manageable, consider the following recommendations:

Plan ahead

Planning ahead in key areas of your life allows you to focus on top priorities and offers you the flexibility to handle those unexpected annoyances that occur during the day.

- Create to-do lists to aid in mental prioritization and to offer a visual sense of accomplishment when tasks are completed.
- Strategize errand running by grouping errands based on location and time.

Establish a backup plan

- Keep a change of clothes and extra shoes in your car or office in the case of a mid-day clothing mishap or an unexpected meeting.
- Before giving a presentation, lessen anxiety by having documents and materials stored on an extra drive, preparing printed copies, and arriving early to familiarize yourself with the meeting room.
- When traveling, avoid booking the last flight of the day to minimize the impact of delays or cancellations.

Set boundaries

- Disconnect from social media, telephone calls, and reading emails after a certain hour in the evening.
- Block time off on your work calendar to catch up on lingering tasks and to accomplish high priority items.
- Follow your instincts and only commit your time and energy to activities that bring you personal or professional satisfaction.

Start with the end in mind

- Wake up and envision how your day will unfold. Commit to sticking to a schedule that aligns with your vision. Limit distractions, worrisome people, and mindless activities that do not fit within your plan.
- Never be late again by properly estimating how long it will take you to complete a task. To arrive at work by 8:30 AM, start in reverse order and think of the preceding activities you must complete. Always give a 20-minute buffer for unexpected occurances:

    Goal: Arrive at Work by 8:30 AM

    Buffer time -20 min
    Commute - 30 min
    Breakfast -15 min
    Get Dressed - 20 min
    Shower -10 min

    Wake-Up: 6:55 AM

- Learn to recognize signs of feeling overwhelmed (e.g.

short-temper, inability to sleep, binge eating, lack of concentration).
- Identify specific needs or tasks that could be handled by a coworker, significant other, or friend.

Maturity, Is That You? How To Recognize You Are Changing For The Better

Have you ever looked at your life two years or even six months back and wondered, *What was I thinking?* or *How did I survive that situation?* If over time you begin to notice that your priorities in life have changed and frivolous things that used to matter seem less important, you may be experiencing a pivotal period of maturity and growth. Although difficult to recognize at first, your transition into a new phase can be a catalyst for re-prioritizing relationships, focusing on your health, or starting a business venture you have been dreaming about for years.

Signs you are heading in a new and positive direction include:

- You are taking steps to improve your finances by saving, cutting expenses, or getting out of debt.
- Your health and fitness become paramount.
- You reward yourself with self-love, quiet reflection, and evenings spent alone.
- The health and wellness of your parents or aging loved ones become more important to you.
- Material possessions become less meaningful, and you seek opportunities to downsize unnecessary clutter.
- You find yourself cleaning out your closet, craving a more functional yet stylish wardrobe.
- Other people's opinions of you become less important.
- You are hesitant to engage in a new romantic relationship until you establish your own value and self-worth.
- You are eager to improve long-term relationships with your spouse, children, or parents.
- You wake up and have a longing to "find yourself."

- New hobbies such as learning a new language, painting, or a practicing a musical instrument bring you great joy.
- You realize the importance of quality over quantity and surround yourself with 2-3 meaningful relationships and friends.

Key Healthcare Numbers to Know

Indicator	What it Means to You	Ranges*
Body Mass Index (BMI)	A measure of body fat based on your weight and height. This metrics is an indicator of overall health and wellness.	Underweight = <18.5 Normal weight = 18.5-24.9 Overweight = 25-29.9 Obesity = BMI of 30 or greater
Blood Glucose Levels (Blood Sugar)	Indicator of the amount of glucose (sugar) in your blood and predictor of diabetes.	For those without diabetes, glucose levels: Before breakfast (fasting) <100 Before lunch/dinner/snack <110 Two hours after meals <140 Bedtime <120
Blood Pressure	Measures the force of blood against the arteries when the heart beats and rests. Consists of two numbers: systolic pressure and diastolic pressure.	119/79 or lower is normal blood pressure. 140/90 or higher is high blood pressure. Between 120 and 139 for the top number, or between 80 and 89 for the bottom number is called prehypertension. Prehypertension means you may end up with high blood pressure, unless you take measures to prevent it.
Cholesterol Levels	Measure of risk factor leading to heart disease, heart attack, and stroke.	Total summation of HDL and LDL: Less than 200mg/dL=desirable 200-239 mg/d=borderline high 240mg/dL and above=high
Pap Smear Results	Measures cervical cells to test for genealogical abnormalities.	Normal results: Normal cervical cells were discovered during your Pap smear. You are said to have a negative result. Abnormal results: Abnormal or unusual cells were discovered during your Pap smear which may indicate a positive result. Relax, a positive result does not automatically mean you have cervical cancer.
Vitamin D Levels	Measures your risk for osteoporosis and bone fractures. Low levels can be a contributor to fatigue, diabetes, cancer, and cardiovascular disease especially among women of color.	20 nanograms/milliliter to 50 ng/mL is considered adequate for healthy people. A level less than 12 ng/mL indicates vitamin D deficiency.

*Always consult appropriate ranges and levels with your provider

Understanding Your Health Insurance

As a young millennial, you may be in the early stages of your career or a seasoned employee considering new opportunities. When you first joined your organization, you may recall signing numerous forms during your first week on the job. In the midst of the chaos, you may have overlooked key details about your employer's benefits offerings and how the plan you selected could impact your level of health coverage. As a millennial woman, it is important to frequently revisit your benefits coverage to ensure adequate coverage. A few topics to understand include:

1. Does your health insurance plan allow you to choose your own doctor without financial penalty?
2. Does your health insurance plan cover visits for mental or behavioral health services?
3. What kind of family planning benefits do you receive? Is fertility assistance included?
4. Does your insurance provider allow more than one Pap smear per year?
5. How much would your insurance premium increase if you were to get married or have a baby?
6. How much maternity leave do you receive and do you have to be employed for a certain time to receive it?
7. Does your company offer a short-term disability policy? Is pregnancy considered a qualifying condition for leave?
8. If you were to become divorced, what are the provisions for taking your ex-spouse/domestic partner off your plan?
9. If you were in an accident, does your plan place a limit on the amount of services it will cover or the number of days you can spend in the hospital?
10. Let's say you lived in North Carolina and had an accident

in Colorado. Would you be required to pay a higher co-pay when visiting the doctor outside of the state you live?

If you cannot answer the majority of these questions, please contact your human resources department or your health insurance company. You should also request a benefits plan handbook for a full overview of your coverage options.

What to Do When Your Medical Information is Incorrect

Picture this scenario: You are stuck in the doctor's office and you take a quick peep at your medical file left visible by the nurse. You notice that your weight is 137lbs when in fact you weigh 143lbs. Do you complain? Probably not!

On a more serious note, what if you read further and determine your doctor listed you as a smoker when in fact you have never touched a cigarette in your life? What if you received a copy of an operative report and found inconsistencies in the information? What should you do? How do you proceed in getting the information corrected?

1. Speak to your provider first and share your concerns.
2. Ask your provider for an official Request/Release of Medical Information form to obtain a copy of your medical records.
3. After receiving a copy of your files, review it with diligence and highlight the disputed information.
4. Ask you provider for a Request to Amend Medical Information form and document your areas of concern.
5. Submit this form along with available documentation to your provider.
6. Keep a copy of your submission for your own records.
7. Note that due to some insurance regulations, certain providers may or may not change or erase the disputed information in your chart.

Finding a New Medical Provider

If you were to receive a bad haircut or a poor manicure, your usual response would be, "I am never going back to that place!"

However, if you received poor service from your physician or delayed communication regarding dreaded test results, it might be harder to break off that relationship due to the effort already spent in establishing it. Regardless of prior efforts, it is important to be satisfied with the clinical expertise and professionalism of your healthcare providers.

Here is the game plan:

1. Talk with your physician or office manager and express your concern.
2. If your physician is receptive to your concerns, consider remaining as a patient.
3. If your concern revolves around poor quality of care, serious medical errors, or an odd personality fit, it may be time to move on.
4. Make sure your insurance company will still cover you if you plan to switch providers and request a copy of your complete medical records to take with you to your new provider.
5. Ask for new recommendations from your friends or use consumer healthcare websites to research the qualifications and patient reviews of potential doctors.
6. After obtaining your records, call your physician or write a professional note outlining your decision to seek medical care elsewhere.

10 Health Symptoms You Should Not Ignore

As millennials, we are used to multi-tasking and putting hard work and other priorities above ourselves. In light of this fact, it is important that we take the time to ensure our health is of key importance and become in tune with our physical wellbeing. If you experience any of the following symptoms, seek medical immediately, as continually ignoring these symptoms could be life-threatening.

1. Unexpected pain in your left arm
2. Sharp chest pain
3. Hair thinning
4. Chronic fatigue and lethargy
5. Unexplained bleeding
6. Chronic headaches
7. Frequent urination
8. A throbbing toothache
9. Tingling toes or fingers
10. Leg pain with swelling

10 Personal Documents to Have Readily Accessible

As a millennial woman, it is paramount that you are in charge of your life and handle your own important life decisions. A key step in this process is making sure you have quick access to personal and medical documents.

1. Birth certificate*
2. Social Security Card and/or Permanent Resident card (if applicable)*
3. Passport*
4. Summary and lab results of your last physical
5. Medical records pertaining to any major surgeries conducted in last 5 years
6. Medical and pharmacy insurance cards
7. Immunization records
8. Documented allergies
9. Documented blood type
10. Emergency contact phone numbers

　*Keep original versions in a safe place.

Skin Care 101

An essential element to any millennial woman's health is proper skin care. Developing a strong and consistent skin care regime, including skin type appropriate products, is key to long-lasting health and beauty. Below is an overview of a standard skin care regime to keep your skin glowing.

Determine Your Skin Type:

Skin Type	Description
Normal Skin	Smooth and firm to the touch: does not get too dry or oily.
Dry Skin	Tight with noticeable areas that flake or peel. Dry skin can look rough and bumpy and seldom gets oily.
Oily Skin	Shiny skin that may produce a residue when touched.
Combination Skin	Skin that tends to get oily in the "t-zone" (area around your nose, chin, and forehead) and dry around your cheeks. Apart from these areas, the rest of the skin is normal.
Sensitive Skin	Sensitive skin often flares, itches, or becomes inflamed in reaction to certain cosmetics, jewelry, or changes in weather.

Use a cleanser designated for your skin type

Using water and a washcloth, clean your face in the morning and prior to bed with an appropriate facial cleanser.

Identify a toner based on your skin type

A toner is a liquid solution designed to balance the pH in

your skin. Use a leave-on toner to help keep skin remain even and supple.

Moisturize often

Use a small amount of moisturizer and apply it to your face and neck. Ensure that your moisturizer aligns with your skin type to prevent clogged pores, whiteheads, or irritation.

Exfoliate weekly

One to two times per week, exfoliate your skin. Exfoliation will remove dead skin cells, leaving your complexion smoother and clearer.

Establish a nighttime regimen

As your skin ages, you may need to consider a nighttime routine, which could include the use of serums for additional moisture, eye creams to remove dark circles, or prescribed creams to keep skin clear.

2. PROFESSIONAL DEVELOPMENT

The key differentiation between a millennial woman who works hard but keeps her head down and one who advances in her career is the strategic use of professional development. Professional development encompasses the hard and soft skills critical to success in the workplace. It additionally provides a competitive advantage due to strong relationship building, development of your personal brand, and the implementation of a strategy for making your expertise valued.

- Building Your Brand
- How to Become a Valuable Employee
- 5 Ways Entry Level Millennial Employees Sabotage Career Progress
- How to Get Introduced to Someone You Professionally Admire
- Navigating a Room… When You Know No One
- 3 Ways to Stop Getting Interrupted When You Speak
- Commanding Respect in a Multi-Generational Workplace: 3 Things Millennial Women Must Know
- The Value of the Informational Interview
- How to Ask for a Letter of Recommendation
- The Art of Following-Up
- Business Cards 101
- How to Join a Board
- 8 Ways to Be a Successful College Applicant

Building Your Brand

What do Apple, Nordstrom, and MAC Cosmetics have in common? They are known for their brands, which include high quality, innovative products, and great customer service. Just like these consumer-driven companies, it is important that you establish a personal and professional brand with your relationships, instructors, clients, and coworkers.

A personalized brand represents the characteristics, attributes, and feelings that others perceive about you and the consistency of your work ethic. Your personalized brand should be positive, strong, and memorable. In order to develop or maintain your brand, implement the following:

Play to your strengths

Identify and build upon your areas of personal and technical expertise, including writing, marketing, strategic planning, project management, relationship building, fundraising, or data analytics.

Promote your skills

Showcase your skills by taking on a stretch role (a role outside of your current position). Offer to support your boss, colleagues, or organizations using your strongest skills.

Demonstrate your value

Create a business case on how your strengths could benefit your employer. For example, if your job could benefit from a streamlined process for tracking feedback from customers, demonstrate how your skill-set can be used to track important data trends, develop a customer service action plan, or increase sales for your company.

Be consistent

The most important aspect of developing your brand is to provide consistent and high level quality of work each opportunity you get. Take pride in your work, presentations, products, or services that you provide. This requires you to pay close attention to detail, ask intelligent questions, meet deadlines, and go the extra mile.

Seek feedback and improve

A key aspect of your brand should include the desire to improve and expand your personal and professional excellence. Seek constructive criticism and real time feedback to obtain an external opinion on your performance and to ensure that your best efforts are being viewed in a positive light.

How to Become a Valuable Employee

While there is no defined "secret sauce" for excelling at work, there is a set of common traits possessed by prized employees. If you are looking to further your brand at work, pursue a promotion, or, if seeking ways to better your performance, include the following in your efforts.

Remain Enthusiastic

- Possess a genuine curiosity and excitement for the work you are doing.
- Remain proactive and always seek opportunities to grow and take on new assignments.
- Keep a positive attitude and remain approachable.
- Participate in social events and networking opportunities.

Be Competent

- Ensure you are viewed as the "go-to" person for a particular subject matter, client relationship, or business area.
- Deliver impactful results on time and remain dependable.
- Keep abreast of current industry topics and news.

Be Entrepreneurial

- Identify a solution first rather than focusing on the problem.
- Take pride in developing and sharing best practices for improvement.
- Put the best interest of the organization before your own self-gain.

Be Self-Reflective

- Welcome constructive criticism and value feedback from others.
- Review previous work deliverables to identify opportunities for self-improvement.
- Put yourself in the place of the employer, client, and co-workers before making decisions.

5 Ways Entry Level Millennial Employees Sabotage Career Progress

1. You always volunteer to be the note taker in team meetings
2. You take too long to follow up on next steps and action items
3. You attend meetings but do not speak or contribute to discussions
4. You haven't mastered how to introduce yourself and nail your elevator speech
5. You are oblivious about workplace politics

How to Get Introduced to Someone You Professionally Admire

As the old adage states, "It's not who you know but who knows you!" One way to expand your personal and professional network is to pinpoint influential individuals in your line of work and social circles. Below are a few steps to make this easier than you realize.

1. Determine why you want to connect with that individual
2. Examine your current network for mutual contacts
3. Ask for the introduction

Here is an example:

"Hey John, I noticed that you previously worked with Alice James at the United Way. I am looking to connect with her and talk about her experience with fundraising. Would you recommend me speaking with her and would you make an introduction on my behalf?"

Using this correspondence:

- You provided clear understanding of why you want to speak with Alice.
- You sought John's opinion and confirmed that Alice is the best person for you to speak with.
- You obtained approval for an introduction.

If John agrees to provide the introduction, ask him to do so via email or in person. You may also reach out yourself and reference John as a mutual contact.

Once the introduction is made:

1. Follow up with Alice
2. Communicate your interest and reason for speaking with her
3. Identify a time or place where you all can connect for 15-30 minutes
4. Remember to follow-up and thank John for his help with a handwritten note or email

Navigating a Room When You Know No One

Whether you are an entry-level employee or a rising executive, work conferences, meetings, and events will be valuable to your professional development. Sometimes, you may attend an event where you do not know anyone. At first, this can be intimidating, but over time, you will realize that these professional events are critical to your success and expanding your network. Gain confidence and work a room in no time with these tips:

- Before arriving, do your research and understand who may be there.
- Dress with confidence and act like you were meant to be there.
- Grab a non-alcoholic beverage and scan the room for friendly faces.
- Find clusters of 3-4 people and introduce yourself.
- Identify common interests with others through small talk.
- Talk for a few minutes and move to your next cluster to network.

3 Ways to Stop Getting Interrupted When You Speak

We have all been there: in the middle of a great point, backed with data and facts and then it hits you like a pigeon squatting on a New York City stoop…you're interrupted! Most likely, this interruption came from a someone who was oblivious of their rudeness, so impatient they lacked restraint from speaking over you, or someone who is threatened by your brain power and uses the interruption as a power dominating move.

No matter the circumstance, it is imperative that you not only correct the wrong done to you but also advocate for your fellow female co-workers in meetings and team sessions.

Here are three quick ways to get started:

1. Acknowledge the wrong quickly

Without missing a beat, quickly turn to the person who interrupted you and try one of these statements:

- "Just one sec, let me finish this point."
- "I have a few more things to add," or
- "John, let me wrap up here."

While this may feel uncomfortable to some, it is critical that you correct the interruption firmly, but politely. You were hired to bring unique value to your employer. By allowing others to continually interrupt your thoughts, you diminish potential innovation, perspectives, and insight that you can offer to your company.

2. Stand when you speak

If the setting allows, stand up to get a strong point across.

Your body language and elevated position of speaking commands respect and makes it less likely for you to be interrupted.

3. Enter discussions with an advocate in the room

No matter the meeting or conversation, aim to have a someone in the room, such as a coworker, who will support you in your talking points, back you up when there are awkward moments of silence, and help ensure that you are not overlooked. Return the favor by making comments such as "Kim, and I were talking about this just last week. Kim, I don't want to steal your idea, why don't you share…"

Commanding Respect in a Multi-Generational Workforce: 3 Things Millennial Women Must Know

Call it what you want—respect, political capital, admiration, or support—the fact of the matter is that when it comes to the workplace, either you have it or you don't.

Millennials make up more than 25% of the workforce. As such, it is highly likely that you work in a multi-generational workforce with co-workers who could be the age of your siblings or even your parents. Working in such as diverse environment requires you to understand various communication styles and master how to gain respect and hold it regardless the person you interact with. Consider the following:

1. Demonstrate Your Competencies First

A bubbly personality, great smile, and well-dressed appearance are valuable in the workplace but those characteristics will quickly dry-up if you lack the ability to demonstrate your competency. Whether you are new to the workforce or seasoned employee, it is critical that you seek opportunities to develop your professional skills. Additional ways to demonstrate your competency include: leading internal training sessions, asking your manager or boss if you can shadow them in meetings or on conference calls, writing whitepapers or articles, taking a lead in a workplace initiative or using social media to share your work place updates with your wider networks.

2. Adapt Your Communication Style

Multi-generational workforces are inundated with various

methods for communication. This includes email, desktop chats, social medial feeds, text messages, face to face meetings, and company intranet sites. To ensure your communications are seen and acted upon, it is important to be aware of the preferred communication styles of your coworkers and team members. Baby boomers often prefer phone calls or face to face communication while millennials prefer texts or emails. During your next team meeting or before your start a major project, confirm communication preferences and outline expectations for keeping everyone up to date.

3. Build Your Network

Gaining and maintaining respect can only be done if have the proper network. Take full advantage of being visible in the workplace and building genuine relationships. Take action by identifying two people each month that you want to get to know better. Depending on your personality, your approach for relationship building may vary. If you are comfortable, set up a coffee chat or lunch date and use the time to learn more about your co-worker. Also remember to be bold and spend time talking about yourself, your personal interests and career interests.

The Value of the Informational Interview

A key step in securing a job often includes reaching out to a colleague or distant acquaintance for an informational interview. Prior to applying for a position, the informational interview is an informal discussion held by the prospective applicant and an employee of the target company.

For prospective applicants, the informational interview permits you to ask "off-the-record" questions, determine your probability of being hired, and gain insider information about issues such as job satisfaction, work-life balance, office politics, and promotion pathways.

Although the informational interview is informal, take it seriously! Too often, prospective applicants fail to recognize the competitive advantage that these interviews can provide and unknowingly remove themselves from being further considered due to lack of preparedness.

Read more to learn about four of the most common mistakes that may prevent you from landing your next job.

1.You Are Not Clear About What You Need

When an employee or acquaintance assists with your job pursuit, it can take upwards of two or more hours of their time. Not only is the person taking the time to speak with you, but they are also reviewing your resume, reviewing the position that you are interested in, and narrowing down the right internal channels to submit your resume. In order to maximize your success, be laser clear on why you are reaching out.

- Do you want more information about the company culture?

- Do you want a review of your resume to determine job fit?
- Are you interested in the career promotion process?
- Are you curious about how the company supports working mothers?

Convey your reason for reaching out and what you seek to gain from the conversation. If applicable, communicate common affiliations such as attending the same undergrad university or mutual acquaintances. This helps to personalize the conversation and can serve as an immediate ice-breaker.

2. You Haven't Done Enough Background Research

The most impressive candidates are those who demonstrate their understanding of the company, industry competitors, and organizational structure.

3. Your Resume Is Not "Easy on the Eyes"

On average, it takes less than 15 seconds to determine if a resume is worth reading further. Before most hiring managers and interviewers dive deep into the content of the resume, they consider the overall formatting and readability of your resume.

Align your resume to the actual job that you seek to perform. Many applicants create only one version of their resume. Given the competitiveness of the job search, it is critical that your resume is tailored to both the position and organization. For example, if you are looking for a job in project management but your resume never contains phrases such as "project management" or "process improvement," this is a red flag.

Your resume should be a truthful reflection of the job posting and demonstrate how your experience meets the needs of the organization. With precision, review the skills and qualifications listed in the job posting. Tailor your resume to include similar words and adjectives as the posting.

4. You Forget Basic Manners

You only get one chance at a first impression, but you get several opportunities to make sure the first impression lasts.

Although handwritten notes leave the strongest lasting impact, following up with a thank you via email is also appropriate and does not go unnoticed.

Asking for a Letter of Recommendation

As you proceed in your professional and academic careers, you will need letters of recommendation to support your application. Letters of recommendation are beneficial when you are applying for:

- Leadership positions
- Study abroad programs
- Placement on a board of directors
- Academic enrichment programs
- Seeking political nomination and appointment

The key to obtaining a positive letter of recommendation is to make sure your recommender understands your positive attributes and to provide them with ample examples of your credentials.

Here are a few steps to consider:

1. Select a recommender who has strong knowledge of your skills over someone with only an impressive title.
2. Ask early and confirm that they will provide you with a positive recommendation. Provide your recommender with sufficient advance notice for writing your letter.
3. Always provide your recommender with your resume.
4. Consider giving written bullet points that highlight your experience and suitability for the position in which you are applying. These points should help your recommender in writing a solid review on your behalf.
5. Give your recommender a deadline for when the letter should be written. This deadline should be at least 2 weeks prior to the actual application deadline. It is often com-

mon for a recommender to forget to write the letter or for the letter go missing. Give yourself enough time to handle these mishaps.

6. If mail submission is required, provide your recommender with a stamped and addressed envelope to ease the submission process.
7. A week before your recommender's deadline, contact him or her to ensure they submitted the letter or to answer any outstanding questions.
8. Follow-up within one week with a handwritten thank you note as a token of your appreciation.
9. If you are selected for the position, be sure to inform your recommender of the good news.

The Art of the Follow-Up

Picture the situation: you have cornered the one person in the room you have been dying to meet. You had a great conversation, secured a business card, and ended the interaction with the so common phrase of "Let's keep in touch!"

Two days…one week…then a month goes by…. You keep reminding yourself to follow-up, but for some reason, you don't! Why is that?

Don't beat yourself up. Often times, the reason that we do not follow-up is out of fear.

This includes the fear of rejection, the fear of not knowing how to initiate the next conversation or the fear of having another to-do added to your list.

Master the follow-up game in the following way:

1. End your conversation by stating, "I would love to keep in touch with you. What is the best way for us to keep the conversation going?" This allows open dialogue and shifts the ownership so that you both are committed to continuing a professional relationship.
2. Make a direct plan, including a time frame and method of communication. Consider this: "Be on the lookout for an email from me at the end of this week."
3. If you prefer email communication, try the following:

Subject: Follow-Up from Chloe Williams at LongLife Fundraiser

Good afternoon, Mr. Kames,

My name is Chloe Williams and we met last Friday at the LongLife

Fundraiser. I enjoyed our conversation regarding your experiences in the marketing industry.

I am starting my career with BigCompany as a Senior Brand Manager. Given our mutual professional interests, I would like to further our conversation, gain insight from your industry experience, and discuss my recent projects.

If amenable, are you available for coffee on Wednesday or Thursday of next week? Please confirm your availability and I will send out a formal calendar invitation.

Regards,

Chloe Williams

Business Cards

Business cards are a critical asset in professional and personal development and networking. Contrary to popular belief, you can also benefit from carrying business cards when you are a student or intern.

If you are either in school or in-between jobs, consider making your own business cards via a local printing company or an online site.

When to Use Your Business Card:

- Anytime you go to a professional event, conference, or workshop.
- When you travel. You may hope that going on vacation is the prime opportunity for you to escape work; however, excellent conversations and professional connections can be made while on vacation or a long plane ride.
- When you are going in for a job interview. Even though you may be interviewing with another company, it is ok and expected to exchange business cards at the end of the interview.

Here are a few quick notes for how to use business cards:

1. Keep your business card to yourself until someone asks for it.
2. Only ask for cards or contact information from people you intend to contact later.
3. Make the most of your networking by connecting with your contacts on a regular basis. On the back of the card, note how you met the person.

How to Join a Board

Serving on a board has the potential to accelerate your career, foster strategic relationships, and provide a fantastic opportunity to serve your community. Here are five tips for kick-starting the process:

Prove your worth

The best assets to boards are members who are valuable in the areas of fundraising, marketing, program development, and community outreach.

Build relationships

Board placement requires the consensus of a selection committee who reviews your professional qualifications but also the value and depth of your personal and professional relationships. Cultivating relationships with existing board members and supporters of your desired organization is critical to selection.

Offer to serve as a junior board member or advisor

If you have yet to build strategic relationships or you are new to a city, one way to contribute to an organization while making a name for yourself is to serve in a non-official role, such as a junior board member, committee lead, or an advisor.

Ensure you understand the responsibilities

Interviewing and speaking with existing board members can be beneficial in ensuring that you understand all the board obligations, such as external fundraising, personal financial pledges, time commitments, and any potential conflicts of interest with your professional employment.

8 Ways to Be a Successful College Applicant

The process for gaining acceptance to college has become more rigorous and competitive. Increasingly, high school graduates are choosing to take a gap year to explore their interests prior to enrolling. While there is no hard or fast algorithm for being a strong college applicant, most college admissions representatives state that early preparation and a commitment to academic and personal excellence is essential.

Whether you are interested in a community college, state school, or top Ivy League, your preparation for college admission should begin no later than your tenth year. Similar to landing a job that requires a strong resume and professional experience, top college recruiters are seeking applicants possessing a documented history of academic achievement, involvement in extracurricular activities, and signs of leadership. Whether you are ready to apply to college or just beginning to identify target schools, consider the following steps to ensure you are well prepared.

1. Create a vision board to visualize your goals and set realistic timelines to achieve them

- Pin-point your career or academic passions early on by identifying other individuals in your family, community, or network that inspire you
- Conduct online research to understand interesting paths and the academic preparation required
- Based on your goals, work backwards and identify the key steps needed for success. For example, if you want to gain admittance to a top 10 college, what are the classes,

prerequisites, and test scores required to be a competitive applicant?
- If a four-year institution is not appealing, consider a community college or vocational school offering a smaller environment or the opportunity to acquire hands-on experience in a shorter timeframe

2. Excel at something

- Find a particular hobby, language, skill, musical instrument, or technical capability that you can master
- Spend your summers and extracurricular time honing that skill-set
- Find unique opportunities such as international summer trips, camps, or enrichment programs that allow you to meet others who share your interests

3. Volunteer

- Share your talent(s) with others by giving back to the organizations that helped mold and shape you
- Offer to join a junior advisory board to influence organizational policies and enhance community outreach

4. Create something from scratch

- Do you have an idea for a unique product or service? Consider creating it!
- Start a club or organization that focuses on a topic that is important to you or needed in your community
- Find friends with similar interests and collaborate with them to bring the cause to life

5. Show your gratitude

- Always acknowledge those who have made an impact in your life
- Have your own personalized stationery to send timely thank-you notes

6. Protect your character

- Be mindful of the types of friends and acquaintances that you keep
- Keep your social media presence very clean! Refrain from posting pictures that show you with alcohol, racially charged images, or where you are dressing provocatively. If you would not want your parent, loved ones, or spiritual provider to see it, do not post it
- Guard your reputation by not engaging in activities that could place you in a negative light

7. Document your successes

- You are never too young to start a resume. No matter your age, start documenting your accomplishments
- Consider creating your own personalized website depicting your passions, academic achievements, travels, and volunteerism

8. Excel academically

- Protect your grades and academic coursework, as they lay the foundation for admissions decisions and scholarships
- If aiming to apply to a top university, pursue rigorous courses such as International Baccalaureate (IB) and Ad-

vanced Placement (AP) level classes to make your transcript stand out
- Explore opportunities in the STEAM (Science, Technology, Engineering, Arts, and Math) fields

3. WORK

In comparison to other countries, the United States puts a heavy emphasis on work culture and career advancement. Our professional occupations dictate many aspects of our lives, ranging from where we choose to live, timing for having children, our personal happiness, and our overall quality of life. Given our society's emphasis on work, the following chapter focuses on how to ensure you land the job you want, succeed at work, and maximize your potential.

- Resume 101
- Top Interview Tips
- Navigating the Interview Process
- Responding to Job Offers
- Non-Compete Agreements 101
- Mastering the First 30 Days of a New Job
- How to Find a Mentor and Sponsor
- How to Ask for a Raise
- How to Take a Vacation and Not Feel Frazzled When You Return
- How to Upward Manage Your Boss
- Handling Workplace Discrimination and Harassment
- 4 Steps to Take After Not Getting Promoted
- Managing an Unfulfilling Job
- Being Laid Off from a Job

- The Art of Delegation and Why You Need to Do It Now
- Resigning from a Job

Resume 101

Your resume is the single most important document to communicate your skills and qualifications for professional opportunitites. Thousands of different online sites will give you advice on how to best structure your resume. Instead of providing formatting and content guidance, here are a few resume dos and don'ts that can help you put your best foot forward.

Resume Dos

- Always convey your most relevant experience for the job or application.
- Review resume for proper formatting, spacing, and consistent font sizes.
- Create more than one version of your resume and be open to tailoring your resume to the specific job.
- Update your resume every 3-6 months based on professional achievements.
- Keep your resume to no more than 2 pages. If you need more space, consider having a curriculum vitae (CV).
- Check the overall formatting of the document by printing a copy of your resume before emailing it.
- Unless otherwise requested, save the resume as a PDF before attaching it to maintain formatting and structure of the document.
- Ensure consistency in how dates are presented (e.g. July 2014-May 2015 or 07/2014-05/2015).
- Start each sentence with a strong verb describing your role or contribution: led, demonstrated, implemented, spearheaded, etc.
- Quantify your value in at least half of your statements. Instead of "Increased customer satisfaction by responding

to client needs," consider "Increased quarterly company customer service ratings by 45% through the resolution of over 150 client requests."
- Use volunteer, internships, and educational experiences if you are short on real work opportunities.
- Consider a 1-2 sentence summary statement that is your resume elevator speech. E.g. "Innovative social media manager with 10 years of Fortune 100 company experience."
- Use a resume template for clean formatting and structure.
- Make sure your email address is respectable and not the address of your current employer.

Resume Don'ts

- Include picture(s) of yourself.
- Use multiple fonts and sizes in the resume.
- Falsely represent or inflate your responsibilities and accomplishments.
- Include information that hints towards your religious, cultural, or political affiliations unless they correlate to the job.
- Use more than 2 lines of text per bullet: keep it short and clear.
- Omit your contact information (Name, email, phone number, city, and state).
- List references on the resume (this wastes valuable space and can be provided upon request of the hiring manager).
- Include a long objective statement. This takes up prime space and adds little value to the reviewing organization or hiring manager.
- Fail to review the job posting and compare it to your resume.

Top Interview Tips

If you were to ask 100 people their suggestions for interviewing, you would receive 100 different answers. Regardless of the number of tips that you receive, there are a few sure-fire tips that you should consider to ensure a successful interview process.

- Research, research, research. Before you apply, perform background research on the organization, the position you are seeking, salary expectations, job benefits, and gather work/life balance feedback from current employees.
- Identify someone at the organization you are interested in to conduct an informational interview with them prior to formally applying. If appropriate, reference your discussions with them as a reason for wanting to seek employment in the organization.
- Dress for the job you want, not the job you have by dressing conservatively and professionally. For most corporate employers, this requires business attire, including a full suit, closed-toed shoes, minimal jewelry, and polished make-up and hair. For positions where there is a relaxed dress code, wear a basic black or navy dress with minimal accessories, such as a scarf or necklace.
- Be prepared to nail standard interview questions including: "tell me about yourself," "why do you want this position?" "why are you looking to leave your current position?" "tell me about a time when you had to lead," and "what are your strengths and weaknesses?"
- Before the interview, determine the name of your interviewer. Research this person prior to your interview and try to find areas of commonality and professional interests.
- When answering interview questions, always aim to

highlight your strengths and the value you'll add to the position.
- Arrive 30 minutes early to the interview. Give yourself 15 minutes to settle in, ensure you have a copy of your resume, and freshen up your appearance. In the final 15 minutes, "check-in" for your interview.
- Bring extra copies of your resume and any non-sensitive work products which demonstrate your capabilities or experiences.
- Ask your interviewer for a business card or contact information. Follow-up with a thank-you note via email and/or a handwritten letter.

Navigating the Interview Process

Depending on the job or organization you are pursuing, you may experience a series of interviews to gauge your fit or skill set. Understanding each stage of the interview process is critical to your success.

First Round Interview

Your first-round interview is your initial contact with the organization. A recruiter or hiring manager may conduct this by phone in order to assess your qualifications.

- Prior to the interview, speak with a current employee to learn more about the organization.
- Reread the job position and make sure that you have a firm awareness of the roles, responsibilities, and skills required for the job. Make sure you highlight your skills during your first-round interview conversation.
- If interviewing over the phone, have your resume in front of you. Be familiar with key achievements on your resume and showcase them during your discussion.
- If being interviewed by phone, find a quiet area with a reliable landline phone connection to take the call.
- Respond to each question with an answer that highlights your skills and value to the organization.
- Respond by answering the question directly. Refrain from long-winded responses and babbling.
- Come prepared to ask two to three questions that relate to the specific position, company culture, or competitive landscape.
- Salary discussions should be initiated by the recruiter. If you are curious about the salary, use online sites to research company and industry salary ranges.

- Do not assume that you are selected for the position or will advance to the next round. Refrain from asking detailed questions about company benefits, vacation policies, or relocation packages unless the hiring manager brings it up.
- Conclude the conversation by asking the recruiter if there is anything else he or she would like for you to answer or share regarding your background or skill set.

Second and Third Round Interviews

Second or third round interviews are geared to determine how you will fit within the company culture and perform in the role. This process may include a phone interview and an on-site interview, where you will interview with potential staff you may manage, your new boss, or team members.

- Prior to the second-round interview, conduct in-depth research to understand the company, the department with which you will be aligned, and the interviewers. Your questions should be tailored to the job in hand, competitors, and how your skills and background will benefit the overall team.
- Likewise, interview with other employees at the company to gain an additional perspective about the organization and the role.
- It is not uncommon for the second-round interview to include more questions that follow behavioral style or case style interviewing. These questions are geared toward understanding your experience in past professional situations and to gauge your subject matter expertise.

Responding to Job Offers

After countless interviews, your phone rings and you receive the offer call you have been waiting for! Before you completely abandon your old job and run for the hills, consider the following steps to ensure your offer is solid.

Acknowledge the Offer

Congrats! Receiving a job offer is a big deal and should be celebrated. Whether you receive the offer via phone or in writing, the first thing that you should do is thank the offering company, and express your appreciation.

Ask for the offer in writing and time to review all details

- Request the offer letter in writing. Key details of the offer letter should include your prospective job title, tentative start date, and initial salary offer.
- Request an overview of the employee benefits package. This provides key information such as allotted vacation days, health insurance coverage, maternity leave policy, and retirement/pension plans.
- After receiving the comprehensive offer package, request time to review the offer in more detail. For example: "Thank you for this offer. I value this opportunity and would like to spend the next 72 hours reviewing all the information provided."
- Remember do not announce the job offer on social media or to your current employer. At this point, you have an offer, NOT the job.

Give Yourself Time to Consider the Pros and Cons

- Compare the salary, benefits, role of the job, and work/life balance factors to your existing job or other offers.
- Seek input from close friends, mentors, and family members.
- Identify any "deal breakers" or factors to make the overall offer more attractive.

Consider Negotiating

- While you should never feel pressure to negotiate, statistics indicate women are paid 30 cents less on the dollar than men for the same position. In addition to pay, factors such as a strong job title, options for telework and vacation benefits should be considered to ensure you are receiving a fair deal.
- If your comparative research indicates you received a favorable offer, then accept. If not, identify what factors, such as salary, vacation time, relocation expenses, and start date, you would like to negotiate.
- Word of caution: Ensure a strong rationale before negotiating. Requesting a $10K pay increase is better negotiated when you can demonstrate objective salary data to support your ask.
- Do not negotiate more than once. Communicate all negotiable requests at one time and in writing.
- If your offer is accepted, great! If not, determine whether it is a deal breaker and move on.

Accept or Decline

- Based on the outcome of your negotiations, either accept

or decline the offer. If you accept, follow the process and timeline requested by the hiring manager.
- If you are going to decline the offer, show respect to the hiring manager by declining via phone with an additional note via email.
- Keep your reasons for declining short but gracious. "I enjoyed learning more about the opportunity at your organization. However, I am pursing another offer that better aligns with my professional goals."
- Note that once you decline, you should not go back to reconsider or renegotiate.

Follow Up with Other Offers:

- After accepting the offer, follow-up with other hiring managers if applicable.
- Inform them that you will no longer be continuing with the hiring process and thank them for their time in reviewing your candidacy.

Non-Compete Agreements 101

A non-compete agreement is a legally binding document held between an employer and employee. The main purpose is to limit employees from leaving the organization to share trade secrets, intellectual property, company processes and other sensitive information with industry competitors. A non-compete is also used to ensure that employees do not use existing company assets (including hardware, software, or other resources) to start their own business and personal ventures.

How Do Non-Competes Work?

Typically, non-compete agreements explicitly prevent employers from working for a competitor for a defined period of time, such as 12-24 months. As an employee, you may be asked by your employer to sign the document and agree to the written terms. Some non-compete agreements may also require you to list any inventions, businesses, patents, or intellectual property that you own.

Who Signs a Non-Compete?

The requirements for who signs a non-compete varies across industries and functional roles within a business or organization. Oftentimes, non-competes are signed by individuals who have a senior position in an organization, individuals who may hold equity in the company, or individuals who are closely affiliated with developing and keeping trade secrets.

Do I Have to Sign One?

If you want the job, the short answer is yes. Generally, employees are asked by their hiring manager or human resources team to sign a non-compete when they are first hired or when they are promoted to a role that meets the company's criteria for having one.

Why Do Non-Compete Agreements Exist?

Non-competes exist to limit direct competition. Put yourself in the place of your employer. If you were the number one company in your field, you would want to ensure that if employees leave your organization, they do not take your company secrets or technical and product development solutions with them. Non-competes also aim to prevent other organizations from easily "poaching" and recruiting employees of competitors.

What Happens If I Leave and Work for a Competitor?

If you do not have a non-compete, from a legal perspective, there is very little concern; however, you may burn political and relationship bridges by working for a competitor. If you do have a non-compete agreement, think carefully before you accept an offer with a competitor. Companies have the ability to bring legal action against both you and the new employer if you break the terms of your non-compete agreement. During your interview process, you should notify the new hiring manager that a non-compete exists, share it with the potential employer, and review the language in detail before making a decision. Conduct additional due diligence by asking your potential employer if they have successfully hired employees from the company you worked for.

Mastering the First 30 Days of a New Job

Starting a new job is exciting, as it offers you the opportunity to get a fresh start within your career. However, after the jitters of a new job wear off, it is time to buckle down, focus on your role, and ensure that your job is all that you hoped it would be. Master the first 30 days of a new job by doing the following:

1. Develop your elevator speech!

During your first few days, you will be asked to introduce yourself, talk about your background, and describe your new role within the organization.

2. Focus on introductions during the first few weeks.

Use team meetings or other group activities to get introduced to new colleagues.

3. Be a social butterfly.

It is tempting to bury yourself in your new office or cubical, but your key focus should be meeting your co-workers and asking them to provide informal introductions on your behalf.

4. Make nice with the administrative assistant or office coordinator.

They will be your lifeline and provide answers to everything from the location of the copier to how you can get a new identification badge.

5. Get boring tasks done first.

In order to be effective in your job, make sure you accomplish the mundane tasks such as payroll and benefits enrollment, email setup, and training requirements early on.

6. Offer your assistance.

Reach out to your boss or team members and volunteer yourself to take on a new project or activity.

7. Do not gossip.

As you are being introduced to new people, it is likely that you may hear both positive and negative comments about other co-workers' personalities, competencies, or work-style. Aim to be objective and keep your opinions and thoughts to yourself until you can form your own assessments.

8. Meet with your manager or boss to outline your roles and responsibilities for the next few weeks.

Use this time to gain and understand how your work will be reviewed and assessed.

9. Exceed expectations.

Based on the conversations with your manager, make every attempt to go above and beyond expectations.

10. Establish a "work best friend" who has worked with the organization for a substantial time.

Schedule informal meetings with them to learn the ins and outs of your workplace.

How to Find a Mentor and Sponsor

Mentorship and sponsorship are two critical concepts to understand as you progress through your professional and personal life. Although often used interchangeably, there are distinct differences between the two and how you should seek both at all stages of your career.

Mentor

A mentor is an individual who may or may not work at your organization but who is still invested in your overall success. A mentor provides strategic guidance and encouragement for your growth and development and helps you create a roadmap for success while serving as a sounding board throughout your life and career.

Sponsor

A sponsor is an individual, often in a higher leadership position, who serves as a tactical advocate and influencer for your long-term career success.

To make this clearer, a mentor is someone who helps you identify professional roadblocks and a sponsor aims and has the power to remove them.

Here are key tips for identifying your next mentor and sponsor:

Make it a natural relationship

- Identify individuals in your workplace or professional circles that you admire and who demonstrate success in their careers.
- Ask them out to coffee or lunch to talk about your industry or mutual topics of interest.

- Refrain from "asking something of them" at that time. Focus on building a genuine relationship.

Be valuable to them

- Offer your mentor or sponsor insight on a topic or assist them with an organizational challenge they may be facing.

Make regular but not too frequent contact

- Set a monthly or quarterly reminder on your calendar to follow-up and check-in with your potential mentor.
- Use the check-in to ask them for insight or feedback on your professional goals and development.

Continue to excel in your career

- In between the times that you are meeting with your prospective mentor or sponsor, make every effort to accomplish success within your job, academics, or personal life.
- Demonstrate you are someone they want to support and advocate for.

Convey your professional appreciation

- During your next meeting, communicate how influential their suggestions and feedback has been in your success.
- Communicate that you consider them to be one of your key career advisors and would welcome the opportunity for them to champion your career growth.

How to Ask for a Raise

1. Assess Your Qualifications
Gather and document your qualifications (e.g. technical certifications, on-the-job training received, advanced degrees, and recent on-the-job successes).

2. Conduct your research
Use online sites and general web searches to determine where your salary and qualifications rank against industry and company averages.

3. Prepare a business case
Combine the research that you have found along with your qualifications and skills to present your rationale for a salary adjustment.

4. Find an opportune time
The best time to ask for a salary raise is right after a positive performance review or when you have been asked to take on additional responsibilities by your manager.

5. Schedule a meeting with HR or your manager
Present your business case and request for salary increase. It is ideal to present this to your HR team since they should remain objective and can provide insight for how compensation is defined in your organization or role.

6. Let your organization propose a number to you.
Rather than stating what specific amount of money will make you happy, use your data and research to show the salary ranges that align with your qualifications.

7. Get the response in writing

If your employer agrees to provide you with a pay raise, obtain the agreement in writing, along with the expected date for the raise to take place.

Even if your employer cannot offer a raise, put your request officially in writing, as you need to revisit the discussion at a later date.

How to Take a Vacation and Not Feel Overwhelmed When You Return

One of the best motivations to get through a stressful period of work is an upcoming vacation. However, it is not uncommon to experience stress in the days leading up to vacation and prior to your return.

In order to minimize any anxiety, here are 12 steps that you can take:

1. A week before your vacation, start to tie up loose projects, time sensitive needs, and responsibilities.
2. Document all projects, responsibilities, or open items that will remain active while you are on vacation.
3. If possible, identify a co-worker who can backfill for you and provide support while you are out.
4. Schedule a meeting with your manager or team leader before your vacation. Review your overall responsibilities and coverage plan.
5. A week before your departure, email important clients, co-workers, and external contacts, informing them that you will be out of the office for a defined period. Ask them if there are things that you can do before your vacation to support them.
6. Two days prior to your vacation, respond to all outstanding emails and voicemails.
7. The evening before your vacation, set up an out of office message for your phone and email. Provide the caller/reader with the date that you will be returning and a contact name for someone who can support them until you are back in the office.

8. Enjoy your vacation and aim not to check email or voicemail until you return.
9. If possible, have your laundry done while you are on your trip. This prevents the need to tackle a dirty load as soon as you arrive home.
10. Plan to arrive home a day before returning to work. Use this time to return personal phone calls, run errands, and mentally gear up for the week ahead.
11. The night before you return to work, spend some time reviewing unread emails received while you were out.
12. Arrive early your first day back. Pace yourself and tackle time-sensitive matters first. It may also be a nice gesture to give those who covered for you a small souvenir!

How to Upward Manage Your Boss

1. Determine your bosses' preferred communication style and use it for sending critical updates or updating them on issues.
2. Understand your bosses' priorities and ensure that your work aligns with theirs.
3. Establish a plan for sharing your progress and work updates.
4. Aim to make your boss shine.
5. Be proactive and meet deadlines earlier than expected.

Handling Workplace Discrimination and Harassment

Although great strides have been made toward gender equality at work and "breaks in the glass ceiling," it is still common for women to rehash stories and traumatic experiences related to work-based harassment and discrimination.

Experiencing harassment or discrimination can make you feel inadequate, angry, hopeless, and confused. While most individuals first think of sexual and racial harassment, women in the workplace are experiencing a rise in career and peer-related discrimination that can take form in the following ways:

- Job advancement sabotage
- Unanticipated role reassignment
- Removal of senior level work responsibilities
- Lack of career promotion year after year
- Preferential favoritism to those who are less qualified
- Workplace "mean girls"
- Managers who use maternity leave as a reason to stall career progression

Addressing workplace discrimination or harassment should be done in a manner that includes well documented conversations and a timeline of events. Consider the following:

Seek third-party input from a trusted co-worker, mentor, or friend.

Assess the situation to ensure what you perceive as discrimination is not a result of miscommunication or underperformance on the job.

If you feel comfortable, communicate your concern directly.

Once you have determined that your work performance has been solid, arrange a time to speak with the individual who is giving you problems. Consider meeting in a public location to lessen any tension.

- Approach the conversation in a professional manner.
- Limit small talk and address your concern head on. For example: "Steve, I wanted us to grab coffee to discuss a comment that you made regarding my appearance last week after our meeting. While you may have meant it in jest, I found it offensive and so did others. We work great together as a team and I wanted to ensure that you were aware of how the comment was perceived."

Document your conversation

Ensure someone other than you and the person who offended you is aware of the conversation. Email your manager requesting time to speak about workplace concern and, if possible, have a face to face meeting to discuss your situation. After meeting with your manager, send a "thank you" note expressing your appreciation for the conversation. Recap the conversation via email, including the outlined steps that your manager recommended for next steps or further conversations with your HR team.

Seek assistance from outside sources

Depending on the level of harassment or discrimination experienced, speak first with your HR team and file a formal complaint. This should be your first step for major offenses such as being called demonizing names or unwanted sexual advances. However, it is important to remember that your HR team works on behalf of your employer. It will often be advantageous to seek professional legal support to ensure that your claim is handled and adjudicated.

4 Steps to Take After Not Getting Promoted

Not getting a desired promotion is a frustrating and professionally painful experience. Instantly, you may take your inability to be promoted personally. You may become jaded with your leadership team or even start to look outside of your organization for other employment. Before you do this, ensure that you are fully aware of why you did not receive a desired promotion and key recommendations for achieving it next year.

1. Request a copy of your performance review and meet with your manager

Spend time reviewing any qualitative and quantitative feedback provided in your performance review. Pay close attention to constructive criticism, any areas of underperformance, and recommendations from your manager. While remaining composed, encourage your manager to deliver the performance review and elaborate on any questions or concerns that you may have.

2. Establish a "business case" for next year's promotion

Based on the areas of professional improvement listed in your performance review and provided by your manager, work collaboratively with your manager to create a business case. This document should reflect, at a minimum, your past professional value and contribution to the organization, key examples of when your work was beneficial to co-workers or other clients, your performance in comparison to internal metrics (e.g. sales goals, # of billable hours, utilization rate, client satisfaction rates), and a descriptive rationale for how your promotion will positively impact your team and overall organization.

3. Increase your professional competencies but also focus on relationship building

Oftentimes, managers, especially men, build relationships outside of the office and in informal ways, such as over sports, cigar bars, and casual drinks. It is not uncommon for women to feel unwelcome in these situations and therefore, lose out on the opportunity to develop key relationships and sponsorship. It is quite possible, although unfortunate, that your leadership team may see your lack of participation and invisibility as a sign that you are not invested or interested in the growth of your career. Equally prioritize workplace relationship building as a tool to grow your brand and increase your chances for promotion. Small efforts such as scheduled coffee breaks, spending more time in the breakroom or cafeteria, or sharing a cab to the airport can help.

4. Communicate your desire to be promoted

This may seem odd, but verbally communicating your desire to be promoted across your management and leadership team is key. Your outward expression not only signals that you are invested in your career and organization, but also holds your manager accountable for your success.

Managing an Unfulfilling Job

Job fulfillment is a top goal that many millennial women strive for in their careers. Feeling unfulfilled is quite common and can impact job performance and personal happiness. Factors leading to job dissatisfaction may include a draining commute, a manager that is incompetent, mindless tasks at work, challenging office politics, or taking on duties that never seem to tap into your personal and professional passions.

While your work environment and superiors may be to blame for your unhappiness, you have the power and ultimate responsibility to improve your situation.

The first step is to have a heart-to-heart with yourself and to unpack what factors are leading to your unhappiness:

- Is there something in your physical environment that can be changed, such as work location, clients, increased opportunity for telework, and more face-to-face time with your leadership team?
- Are you bringing your full self to the table?

    † Are you "checking out?" Do you avoid happy hours, lunches, and other team building activities? Why?
    † Is there something in your personal life distracting your attention and full energy from your work?
    † Are you facing a health issue or personal stresses at home hindering your full performance?

- Are your leadership team and mentors at work aware of your concerns?

    † Have you had professional development sessions with

your leadership team or managers to talk about suggestions for improvement?
† Have you sought counsel from other co-workers or friends in other industries?

- Do you have the right skills needed to take your job/career to the place you desire? Have you:

  † Assessed if you are qualified and capable of handling a promotion?
  † Deciphered the difference between your "internal desires" for a promotion versus your actual readiness?
  † Identified 4-5 tangible differentiators that make you qualified for more responsibilities?
  † Sought a stretch role to test your ability to take on more senior work?

After addressing some of the questions above, identify specific factors that can be changed to improve your satisfaction.

- Do you need more responsibilities? A different team? A more structured work environment? Enhanced mentorship? A career that includes international travel? Increased compensation?
- If you can pinpoint key drivers that will make you happier and more fulfilled, first focus on seeking those things within your current employer. Remember, the grass is not always greener, and you should never make a permanent decision on temporary feelings.
- Explore your true passions through volunteering and extracurricular activities. For example, if your dream is to become a top photographer, but you are a bank teller, pick

up work on-the-side until you can make a full transition to your desired career.

If you determine that your current job is affecting your mental and/or physical well-being and no longer provides value to your intended career path, it may be time to look elsewhere.

- First, seek family and/or spiritual guidance.
- Start speaking to mentors or others who are in the career field/positions that you seek.
- Utilize alumni job databases and online professional social media sites to ask for warm introductions and informational interviews.
- Spruce up your resume and start filling in the gaps if you need additional skills or credentials.
- Ask for referrals via friends and professional colleagues.
- Be patient and purposeful about your search.

Being Laid Off from a Job

Whether you are aware of a potential layoff or it comes as a complete surprise, facing unemployment can be traumatic, stressful, and nerve-wracking. However, having a game plan for how you will handle your unemployment may offer peace of mind.

If your layoff is expected, get your affairs in order as soon as possible.

- Begin conversations with your HR managers to ensure that you are getting everything that is due to you, including severance pay, vacation, and sick leave payouts.
- Negotiate a benefits package.
- Understand your options for continuing your healthcare insurance.
- Request a positive letter of recommendation for future job searches.
- If needed, register for state unemployment benefits.
- Allow yourself ample time to review all paperwork that your employers may provide pertaining to the layoff. Do not sign anything until you have had time to review your options.

Prepare yourself financially

- Prior to your last day at work, begin to set a financial budget and determine what impact the layoff may have on your finances.
- Cut back on unnecessary expenses such as eating out, clothing splurges, and weekend entertainment.
- Mourn the loss of the job but realize that you must move on.
- Try to remember that the layoff was not personal.

Rediscover your interests

- Use the time off to determine your true professional passions.
- Explore volunteering opportunities in line with your job of interest to gain additional experience.

Rebrand yourself

- Brush off your resume and update the content with recent skills and qualifications gained from your past employment.
- Identify technical skills or capabilities needed for your next desired position and use the time off to build those skills.

Reach out to your network

- Once you identify a few potential ideas for your next opportunity, start reaching out to your personal and professional network.
- Be honest about your layoff and use networking as an opportunity to explore job referrals and warm leads.

Give yourself time

- Keep your confidence up. Layoffs often have more to do with the management and operations of the company rather than your personal performance.

The Art of Delegation and Why You Need to Do It Now

Delegating work is a critical tactic for achieving career success and a manageable work/life balance. Many women report that as they rose to the top of their careers, their level of responsibilities increased, but the work actually became easier due to their ability to delegate. Delegation is a must do for millennial women who pride themselves on having multiple responsibilities.

Here are 4 ways to ensure you delegate successfully.

1. Be Clear on What Needs to Be Done

In order to manage others and ensure that work is done, you must have a clear understanding of what needs to be done. This often requires that you have strong planning and communication skills to effectively convey a vision and plan of attack to others. When it comes to work, most individuals pay too little attention to the planning phase and therefore approach a task or responsibility without a clear path forward. This often results in confusion across roles, lack of clarity regarding the goal, and misunderstandings pertaining to important timelines and details. Prior to delegating tasks, spend time understanding what support you need, identify who in your company or team can support you based on their level of expertise, and determine where to hold face-to-face meetings to discuss roles, responsibilities, and timelines.

2. Build a Strong Team

As the age-old adage goes, "You're only as strong as your weakest link." It is important that you establish team members, partners, collaborators, and staff who can execute efficiently on the tasks and responsibilities assigned to them. These individuals should be highly skilled in completing their area of work, not necessarily skilled at managing the whole project.

3. Limit Micro-Managing the Team

The ultimate benefit to delegation is that after you have communicated what work needs to be completed and identified strong team members, you now have the ability to let the work happen while you focus your attention on more critical or time sensitive responsibilities. Many leaders fail to recognize this as a strategic asset and rather, view the ability to delegate only about power and control. In order to delegate, you need to establish and communicate periodic check-points with your team members and outline when milestones should be hit and when you will be communicating with them to confirm the quality of their work product and responsibilities. Your team should know that you are there for them in case of urgent questions and assistance, but they should also understand that after expectations have been communicated, you will give them the liberty and latitude to work independently.

4. Review the Work and Provide Real-time Feedback

Once your team members have completed their responsibilities, take time to independently review their work. Gather comments that you will use to provide feedback on the quality, timeliness, and accuracy of their work. Offer positive and constructive real-time feedback so your team members are well aware if they met your expectations or where they fell short. Your original project timeline should have included sufficient time to provide feedback and allow for revisions of work. If for some reason the work or action requested is not correct, be clear in what the next steps should be and provide a strict timeline for finishing the work. If necessary, allocate additional resources, such as other team members, to assist. The last and least favorable option should be for you to actually do the work or fix errors.

Many new managers and leaders struggle with the idea of letting others do the work when they believe they can "get it done faster." Although this may be true, doing the work for your team completely eliminates that value and the strategy of delegation. Performing the work for your team is actually a negative reflection of your ability to lead and manage. It signals that you did not plan appropriately to begin with, you did not have a strong team, or you under-communicated expectations.

Resigning from a Job

Deciding to resign from a job can stir many emotions and possibly, feelings of discomfort. In some instances, you cannot wait to leave your old employer, and you can only dream about your last day. In other situations, the decision to leave is bittersweet, since you formed long-standing relationships and had a great experience with your employer.

Regardless of your situation, the most important goal is to resign with class and professionalism.

Here is the process for resigning:

Do not announce your intent to resign until you receive the following items from your new potential employer:

- A written and signed job offer between you and the hiring manager. The offer should include a start date, salary, any negotiated offer terms, completed verification of background check, and employment eligibility.
- An understanding of job benefits, including health, insurance, retirement, and vacation.
- A thorough review of any non-competes and confidentiality agreements to ensure that your new role is not in violation of your prior position.
- Re-confirmation from the hiring manager that all hiring documents are in place and you are hired.

Determine your last day of work

Industry standards suggest providing a two-week notice. However, if you are in a senior position or your job is specialized, it would be gracious to offer more time.

Prepare your "exit story" and transition plans

Prior to meeting with your boss, prepare a solid explanation for why you are leaving. Note that your explanation should exclude things that you disliked about your last job. Rather, communicate that you are seeking new opportunities for professional growth, new industry experience, or you are pursuing educational opportunities. Regardless, it needs to be a positive spin on the situation.

Tender your resignation by meeting with your boss

If you and your boss are not in the same location, a phone conversation is suitable. During this time, discuss your transition plan and offer your time to cross-train the new person taking your position. Tie up any loose project ends before your last day. Also, extend gratitude and appreciation for your time with the company.

Send a formal resignation letter to both your boss and your HR representative.

After meeting with your direct manager or HR representative, send a formal letter. This letter should be brief and communicate your appreciation of the employment opportunity, and includes the date of your last day of employment.

- Notify co-workers, leaders, and mentors who had a substantial impact on your career about your upcoming transition.
- Prior to your last day, clear your workspace of personal items. Follow your company's guidelines regarding transfer and storage of electronic documents and files.
- If you amassed presentations, deliverables, important emails, and projects during your time at your job, note that

you make not be entitled to take the documents with you. Legally, the documents are often owned by your company.

Send final thank you and notification emails to co-workers and clients.

- Include your personal email address and contact information for long-term follow-up.
- Wait 3-4 weeks after resigning before you update on-line professional profiles with your new company name and position.

In addition to sending your resignation letter, be mindful of the following:

- Never confuse a job offer with actual employment. An offer can be withdrawn at any moment.
- Your current employer may offer you more money or a promotion to stay. This offer seldom turns out well. Be prepared to decline.
- Coworkers and HR will ask where you are going. Respond by stating, "Things are still in the works, but I will remain in the industry."
- Be prepared to be escorted out. Depending on your industry, security may ask you to pack up, turn in your badge, and walk you out of the building.
- Be prepared for your boss and other co-workers to keep you at a distance once you communicate your resignation.
- Work hard until the last hour. A resignation does not grant you the privilege to slack off and coast. Continue to provide value.

4. RELATIONSHIPS

Personal relationships are the glue that hold our lives together and give us inspiration. These relationships can take place in many forms and include strong friendships with other women, connections with significant others, and day-to-day relationships with new and longstanding acquaintances. As we get older, we often find that the value of these relationships become more important but harder to maintain. Work, personal responsibilities, and family needs can interfere with our ability to keep these relationships going and meaningful.

- How to be a Great Friend
- What to Do if Your Friendship Circles Clash
- 7 Tough Conversations to Have with Yourself Each Year
- Outgrowing Friends
- Cohabitation with a Significant Other
- Making a Great First Impression
- 10 Reasons You Should Think Twice Before Marrying
- How to Be a Great Bridesmaid
- How to Be a Great Party Host
- 5 Easy Ways to Perform Acts of Kindness

How to Be a Great Friend

As you get older, your friendship circles will change, as true friends come few and far between. Regardless of how others have treated you, always take the high road and aim to be a great friend to those you value. Here are a few things to consider:

Let your friends know that you are available

The best friends are those that you can go periods of time without speaking and within seconds reconnect like the conversation never ended.

As life moves along, women face an enormous number of challenges, including changing jobs, marriages, divorces, pregnancies, miscarriages, depression, entrepreneurship, and mid-life crises.

These events can take their toll and at times cause us to retreat from life. No matter what your friend is going through, it is important to allow them the space they need, but check on them periodically to express that you are available for support.

Want the best for your friends

Your friends are an extension of you, and therefore, you should always want the best for them and support their pathway to success. True friends do not compete with one another but rather encourage and cheer each other on.

Support your friends by connecting them with other friends of yours in the same line of work, sharing relevant news articles or events that may be of interest to them, and encouraging them to succeed.

Be low maintenance

Being a great friend should be effortless. If you find yourself to putting on a mask, aiming to dress better, or trying to out-do your friend just to spend time with them, you should reevaluate your relationship.

Sense when your friend needs help

Do not abandon your friend in their greatest time of need, and recognize when to pull in additional support when needed. Often times, your friend may be too overwhelmed or even prideful to ask for help. This is when you should step up to the plate and help them out, whether they need a meal cooked, childcare, or assistance preparing for a major presentation they have coming up.

Be dependable and consistent

One of the best traits a great friend can possess is dependability. Life often presents unexpected situations that do not allow for adequate preparation and planning. If your friend demonstrates that he or she needs support, provide consistent and dependable support by visiting or calling, taking your friend to doctor's appointments, helping plan a wedding, or helping them move into their new home.

Know when to apologize

Being a good friend also means knowing when you may have made a mistake or offended your friend. It is important to acknowledge when you make a mistake and apologize.

Recognize when to mind your own business

As a close friend, you will be privy to personal and confidential details of your friend's life, such as details about their finances, job, marriage, and family dynamics. It is not uncommon for your friend to share information with you that may disagree with or have a strong opinion about.

Although you should always act in the best interest of your

friend's wellbeing, there will come times when you need to remain neutral, objective, and silent. Unless there are signs of physical, verbal, or mental abuse or another situation that may be detrimental to your friend's health, try not to interfere directly with his/her romantic relationships, career, or business decisions.

When Your Friendship Circles Clash

If you watch any amount of reality TV, you may think it is acceptable for women to engage in excessive gossip, backstabbing, and physical altercations.

The reality is that most women have distinct and healthy circles of friends established from childhood, college, work, or other personal networks. It is not uncommon for these circles to intersect and lead to the expansion of deep and meaningful relationships.

However, there are times when select individuals in your circles will not get along. For the most part, that is OK, but when it comes to "shared events" such as weddings, parties, family trips, and baby showers, you want to make sure that you do your part in keeping the peace.

Here are a few tips to consider:

Refrain from degrading one friend when speaking with others

It is OK to acknowledge that your two girlfriends may not see eye to eye, but never gossip or consent to negative discussions.

Always inform your friends who will be coming to a party or event

Never surprise your friends by having the ex-girlfriend or a former bestie meet without prior notification.

Set expectations

Communicate that you honor both of their relationships and ask them to play their part in keeping the peace.

Reevaluate friendships

Spend some time reflecting and determining if the person

who causes conflict or chaos in your friend circle adds or subtracts value from your life. It may be time to go your separate ways.

7 Tough Conversations to Have with Yourself Each Year

1. Do my financial spending and savings habits support my long-term personal and professional goals?
2. Do my current friends provide me with the support I need in this stage of my life?
3. Would I be happier and more fulfilled with a career change?
4. Do I prioritize my healthcare and personal wellbeing?
5. Are there relationships with loved ones or family members that need repair or closure in order for me gain peace of mind?
6. Is there something holding me back from my full potential?
7. What life lessons am I grateful for this year?

Outgrowing Friends

Ah, friendship! The concept of friendship is ingrained in all of us from the time we are toddlers. For the most part, we are taught to cherish our friends, be nice, be loyal, and do unto others as we would want done unto us. However, we are seldom taught to recognize the signs of a stale friendship and how to handle it with ease.

Most women who are seasoned in relationships and life understand that outgrowing friends is a natural and necessary occurrence in living your best life.

Signs of outgrowing friendship include:

- You and your friend bicker more often than usual
- You recognize that your friend's maturity level is not aligned with yours
- Your friend drains your energy, emotions, or finances
- You find yourself ignoring their phone calls and text messages
- Your friendship no longer uplifts you
- You find it difficult to talk about multiple aspects of your life (work, relationships, and personal goals)
- You sense that your friend is in competition with you

If you notice one or more of the signs, have a direct conversation about your emotions. If you decide to pull away, take some time to determine if the withdrawal makes you feel better. If so, it may be time for you to invest your energy elsewhere.

Cohabitation with a Significant Other

Like it or not, cultural views of cohabitation and sharing spaces with significant others have changed. Many times, couples decide to live together for financial reasons or because they have an existing family. If you make the decision to cohabitate, it's important to make sure that you understand the ups and downs and how to make the best of your decision.

Discuss finances early and often

Whether your decision is to split finances 50-50, based on percentage of income, or some other mechanism, it is important to discuss finances early on. Arguments based on finances are not only the number one cause of dissolution of romantic relationships, but also the ending of personal friendships and business partnerships. It is important that an open dialogue is held about how you will spend money and who will be accountable for paying for certain household expenses.

Maintain high levels of personal hygiene at all times

This includes bathing and cleaning up after yourself on a regular basis. Establish a schedule for bathroom cleaning and personal care. If space allows, keep your belongings and personal items, such as tampons, sanitary pads, hair care and other personal products, organized. Establish open communication about expectations for daily or weekly cleaning processes for shared living spaces and household chores such as sweeping, vacuuming, and daily cleaning of the dishes.

Create your own personal space

Living together can be fun and enjoyable, but it can also be very stressful for both individuals. Make sure you establish pleasant spaces to enjoy downtime and self-care.

Discuss distribution of domestic duties

Our expectation of what our significant other, spouse, or mate should do is often based on what we saw depicted as children. It's unreasonable to expect the person you live with to read your mind and to understand your expectations for cooking, cleaning, and financial management. Regardless of what society tells us about gender specific household roles and responsibilities, it's up to you and your significant other to decide what works best for you and to divide and conquer based on each of your strengths.

Communicate and understand each other's socialization habits

Are you a homebody who enjoys closing the shutters at 7 PM and snuggling up with a good cup of hot tea? Is your spouse or significant other someone who enjoys having friends and family over and would welcome someone dropping by at 11 PM? If possible, establish rules or expectations about socialization preferences to limit frustrations among both of you.

Making a Great First Impression

Whew! You've met your significant other's family. Meeting the family should signal that you and your love interest are taking it a step closer in your relationship. Understand the dos and don'ts when meeting the family to win them over!

Be well dressed

Make a great first impression by dressing better than the occasion. Ensure your attire is age appropriate but conservative.

Be thoughtful

- Bring a gift for your hosts. An inexpensive gift, such as flowers, a candle for mom, or a family gift, such as baked desserts, makes a lasting impression.
- Make sure that you and your significant other's stories of how you met are aligned.
- Be sociable. Although it may be overwhelming, engage with all members of the family and be open to conversation.
- Even though your significant other's family may make jokes, do not make negative comments about your significant other.
- Offer to be helpful if there is food served or during cleanup.

Be conservative

If you are staying overnight, sleep in separate rooms. Also, make sure you have packed decent pajamas.

Be gracious

Send or leave a thank you note for the hospitality shown to you.

10 Reasons You Should Think Twice Before Marriage

Marriage is very rewarding but is ultimately hard work. Before making the commitment, it is important to have a conversation with yourself and understand your desires and maturity. Here are a few things that, if unresolved, may impact your readiness for marriage:

1. You carry unresolved issues due to previous relationships, a traumatic childhood, or other destructive events.
2. Your finances are unstable due to significant debt, inconsistent income, or constant overspending.
3. You lack a spiritually-rooted motivation for desiring a spouse.
4. Your past includes strained relationships with close family members, siblings, or friends.
5. You have a general sense of mistrust in people.
6. You like your partner but hope that marriage will improve certain characteristics of their behavior.
7. You carry deep-rooted secrets that you are ashamed to communicate.
8. You are battling an unmanaged mental health issue.
9. You are scared to commit due to challenging relationships with your parents or close family members.
10. You lack ample self-love and self-esteem and are looking for a spouse to compensate.

Relating to these issues does not mean that marriage is off the table. However, these red flags often lead to difficult relationships if they are not addressed and handled. Consider seeking appropriate pre-marital counseling or therapy if you are unable to resolve one or more of these issues alone.

How to Be a Great Bridesmaid

Receiving an invitation to serve as a bridesmaid is an honor and privilege. However, the responsibility of your role can be exhausting, expensive, and a heavy time commitment. Consider the following to make the process enjoyable and pleasant!

Decline the offer

If you will be strapped for money, time, or facing another life commitment, such as being pregnant during the wedding, it is ok for you to decline and offer your services as a co-planner or hostess.

Realize this is not your day!

As a bridesmaid, you help make important decisions such as choosing the wedding dress, favors, wedding colors, and entertainment. Although withholding judgment may be difficult, try to support the bride's decisions and not promote your own personal interests.

Help reduce drama

A wedding can be one of the most stressful events a bride will face due to the coming together of families, managing of the wedding budget, and dealing with unruly guests. As a bridesmaid, you should help handle the chaos. Shield the bride from mind-numbing bickering, pestering from her future mother-in-law, and stressing over final touches. Never complain to the bride and aim to keep her cool and calm throughout.

Be helpful!

Ask any bride and she will tell you about bridesmaids who did not carry their weight throughout the wedding preparation process. Be helpful by making favors, serving as a host/co-host for bridal showers, helping the family pack up gifts after the wedding, preparing the bridal suite, helping her create her bridal registry, and assisting with the preparation and management of invitations.

Stay sober

As a bridesmaid, your day will start early and end late. You will be hungry and you will be drained. As tempting as it may be, cocktail hour does not signal the end of your duties as a bridesmaid. Refrain from over indulging in alcohol and embarrassing yourself and or the bride. Keep yourself together, as you never know when you may need to be there for the bride!

How to Be a Great Party Host

The key to being a fantastic party host is to put yourself in the position of your guests! From the moment your guests are invited to your event to how they feel when they leave, your party should be planned and executed with great detail. The second rule is to ensure your guests do not see you flustered! Make every attempt to plan your event with ease so that you can enjoy your party too. Here are a few additional tips for planning a festive event:

1. Depending on your budget, consider using a party planner to assist you in planning, executing, and handling unexpected events.
2. Ensure invitations provide clear directions and instructions for details including attire, parking, door entry codes, and a contact number.
3. Organize the event's space or your home furniture in a manner that encourages conversations.
4. Ensure common areas such as bathrooms are well stocked and able to accommodate frequent usage.
5. Greet each guest and thank them for coming.
6. Consider having a co-host to support details such as food preparation, music, favors, and set-up/break-down.
7. Plan with diligence your food and beverage needs to prevent running out and having unfed guests.
8. Keep food and drink accessible for guests.
9. Make sure your entertainment choices keep the party going.
10. Encourage introductions for guests who arrive alone or may not know anyone else at the party.
11. Place trash cans or dirty dish disposal stations throughout your party to prevent guest from bottlenecking by one location.

12. Provide multiple areas for guests to enjoy themselves and have quiet conversations.
13. Enjoy yourself! Take time to eat, drink, and engage with your guests.

5 Easy Ways to Perform Random Acts of Kindness

1. Send a long-lost acquaintance a bouquet of flowers or a card to express that you are thinking about them.
2. Bring a small souvenir back from one of your vacations to your friends or co-workers.
3. Place a bottle of water in your mailbox for your mail person on a hot day.
4. Take a holiday gift to often "invisible" service providers such as cleaners, nail technicians, valets, office janitorial staff, doctor's office staff, or pharmacy staff.
5. Pick up the tab for the person or family behind you at a coffee shop or drive-thru.

5. FINANCES

Poor handling of finances and the lack of financial planning early on can be detrimental to the success of millennial women. This chapter offers key tips for financial health and sound money management.

- Top Financial Mistakes Millennial Women Make
- 10 Financial Tools that Every Millennial Woman Needs
- What is an Emergency Fund?
- Why Financial Autonomy is Critical for Millennial Women
- Monitoring Your Credit
- How to Start Investing with Any Income Amount
- How to Pay Down Debt
- Handling a Declined Card
- Maximizing Your Earning Potential
- Pre-Nup or Nope?
- Staying in Control of Your Money
- 5 Reasons to Start Advanced Planning Now
- Financial Tips for College Bound Millennials
- Living a Champagne Life on A Beer Budget

Top Financial Mistakes Millennial Women Make

1. Failing to focus on retirement during earlier working years
2. Ignoring financial hardships rather than tackling them head on
3. Allowing financial stress to affect personal health
4. Staying in debt too long
5. Assuming that homeownership is unattainable
6. Not saving for personal goals and dreams such as starting a business or reinventing a career
7. Overspending on material items
8. Failing to partner with other women to trade services, such as tax help, in exchange for business marketing assistance
9. Undervaluing yourself at home, in the work place, or when doing business with customers
10. Not remaining in control of your personal finances after marriage or romantic partnership

10 Financial Tools that Every Millennial Woman Needs

1. An emergency fund of no less than $1000
2. A checking account held solely by you
3. A savings account that contains at least 3-6 months of living expenses
4. A strong credit score
5. A retirement investment account
6. Life insurance
7. A current will
8. Disability insurance
9. Adequate health insurance
10. An affordable and trustworthy financial advisor

What Is an Emergency Fund?

An emergency fund is a separate account accessible in the case of an emergency only. Such emergencies are expenses you did not budget for but are necessary for your basic need of shelter, food, transportation, and health.

Such expenses may include unexpected car repairs, a broken home air conditioner, or medical fees for urgent care. The emergency fund is NOT to be accessed when you run low on money and fail to budget. It should also not be used for discretionary purposes such as shopping, hair care, or vacations.

For most individuals, $1000 should be the minimum amount within your emergency fund. Fund this account first before setting additional money aside for savings.

Why Financial Autonomy is Critical for Millennial Women

Domestic partnerships and marriages offer couples the opportunity to combine resources and collectively build a successful future. In spite of this fact, disputes pertaining to finances are the leading cause of divorce and separation.

Although it is not uncommon for one individual to make more money than the other, it is important that the relationship allows financial autonomy for both persons. Many women report that financial dependency on a partner is a key factor in long-term unhappiness or the decision to stay in abusive relationships.

All too often, well-intentioned women enter relationships without having critical financial discussions and find themselves in situations where money is used as leverage to control, manipulate, and manage their lives.

It is important that if you are ever in a personal need or crisis, you have unobstructed access to cash. This cash should be saved in a separate account and accessed only if you need to independently support yourself or dependents for an extended period of time.

Monitoring Your Credit

Your credit score, also called a FICO score, is a three-digit number ranging from 350 to 850. This score represents your past financial behavior and help creditors to understand your likelihood to manage and repay debt.

A FICO score of 750 to 850 is excellent, and those with a score in that range have access to the lowest rates and best loan terms. Scores between 700 and 749 are good and individuals in this range may get loan approval while paying a higher interest rate. A score of 650 to 699 is fair, and those with a score in this range will pay higher rates or could even be declined for loans and credit.

The information reported on your credit reports comes from three bureaus: Experian®, Equifax®, and TransUnion®. Five main factors are included to determine your credit score:

Payment history (35 percent)
This category reflects your account payment history, including any delinquencies and public records.

Amounts owed (30 percent)
Reflects how much available credit you have compared to debt across all accounts.

The length of credit history (15 percent)
Reflects the age of your credit accounts and the frequency of usage.

Types of credit used (10 percent)
This category considers the mix of revolving and installment accounts you have open.

New credit (10 percent)

Assesses the amount of new credit provided, including credit inquiries and number of opened accounts.

In addition to impacting your ability to qualify for a car loan, mortgage, or credit card, your credit score can also be used to approve or deny applications for cell phone plans, utility services, and employment.

If you have a less than desirable credit score, there are some ways to improve it. However, the biggest factor for improving your score is time. Here are a few additional tips to make sure your score stays strong:

1. Pay your bills on time and avoid having bills sent to a collector.
2. Refrain from adding irresponsible family members or love interests on your credit or loan accounts.
3. Be cautious if someone asks you to co-sign on a loan. You are responsible if they default on payment. Be cautious of opening multiple credit cards and accepting offers in a department store just for a percentage discount.
4. Keep credit card debt to less than 30% of your total available credit. For example, if you have a total of $10,000 in credit available to you, try not to carry more than a $3000 balance at a time across all your accounts.
5. Refrain from "maxing out" credit cards or going over your balance limit.
6. Do not ignore speeding or toll tickets. They can appear on your credit report if unpaid.
7. Use credit with caution. Having no credit cards or inactive lines of credit can also impact your score.
8. Check your score often. Contrary to popular belief, checking your credit score with a credit score vendor does not always lower your overall score.

How to Start Investing with Any Income Amount

Investing is the process of setting money aside for long-term gain. This includes taking a risk that your money may lose value at times but also may realize gains in the future. Here are a few ways to begin investing no matter how much money you have:

Take advantage of your workplace retirement plan

About half of all US employers offer a retirement plan allowing you to contribute pre-tax contribution dollars to a retirement fund. Many employers also offer dollar for dollar matching up to a certain percentage. Speak with your HR team to gain more information about enrolling.

Establish a 529 College Savings Plan

A 529 Plan is an education savings account operated by a state or educational institution designed to help families set aside funds for future college costs. It is named after Section 529 of the Internal Revenue Code, which created these types of savings plans. With less than $20 per month, you can invest money into the plan. Most often, the beneficiary is a child, grandchild or younger relative. However, an adult can also open a 529 plan to save for his or her own higher education costs since there are no age limits.

Open a Roth Individual Retirement Account

Even if your employer does not offer a retirement plan, you can obtain one through a reputable financial advisory company and fund it yourself. A Roth IRA is a great place to start! A Roth IRA is an individual retirement account that allows you to contribute after-tax dollars to your fund. After-tax dollars reflect the net income that you take home after all federal and state taxes have been removed. Roth IRA rules dictate that as long as you've owned your account for 5 years and you are age 59½ or older, you can withdraw your money when you want to and you will not owe any federal taxes. Other advantages of the Roth include no required minimum distributions, no age limit for contributing, and no tax penalties to your beneficiaries.

How to Pay Down Debt

Have you ever had a bill that seems to stay around forever even though you are making payments? To make traction and to get out of debt, you need an action plan to prioritize your debts.

One suggestion is the debt avalanche method where extra cash is dedicated to paying debts, starting with the smallest amount owed. As each smaller debt is repaid in full, the money previously used to pay that debt that month is then applied toward making additional payments on the next-smallest debt, and so on until all debts are repaid.

1. On a piece of paper, write down your debts smallest to the largest by dollar value.
   Bill 1-$25 cell phone
   Bill 2-$59 electric bill
   Bill 3-$295 credit card
   Bill 4-$1940 medical bill
2. Calculate the minimum amount you can make on all payments other than bill #1.
3. When budgeting for monthly payments, your budget will be the minimum payment for debts bills #2 through #4 plus the entire amount (or manageable portion) of bill #1; keep doing this until bill #1 is paid off.
4. Once bill #1 is paid, pay the minimum amount on the remaining debts while adding the extra $25 that you now have to bill #2.

Handling a Declined Card

Far too often, shoppers make the mistake of keeping a mental tab of checking account balances and run into trouble due to poor accounting.

Whether because of poor budgeting or a technical glitch, we all have experienced or witnessed the awkward moment of a declined card. How you handle yourself in this situation can minimize your embarrassment.

1. Going forward, make sure you have enough money in your account and become aware of daily limits set by your bank.
2. If in your gut you know that you do not have the money, ask the cashier to place your items aside and apologize for the error. Leave the store.
3. If there could be a mistake, ask the cashier to try your card again.
4. If the card still does not work, suspend your transaction, step aside, and call your financial institution.
5. Once the issue is resolved, thank the cashier for his patience and resume your purchase.
6. If the purchase cannot be made, apologize for the error and leave the store.

Overall, refrain from making excuses for what could have happened, acting flabbergasted, or becoming belligerent about your situation.

Maximizing Your Earning Potential

Cost cutting is often the first action individuals take as a means to have more money each month. While cost cutting is important, also pay attention to your earning potential. Consider the following:

- Are you earning top dollar based on your qualifications and skill set?
- Are there other skills, certifications, or degrees that you need to boost your salary?
- Should you seek an external position so you can negotiate a better salary?
- Do you have a creative talent that can be used to produce a product or service?
- Have you considered selling your crafts or services at a local farmers market or on e-commerce sites?
- Do you have flexibility in your schedule that allows a part-time job such as tutoring, piano lessons, or sales?
- Do you find yourself being the go-to person for a particular topic or subject matter? Can you monetize your knowledge?
- Is it time for you to start your own business while using the stability of a full-time job to fund your passion?

Pre-Nup or Nope?

A pre-nuptial agreement (pre-nup) is a legal contract between two spouses that establishes the property and financial rights of each spouse in the event of a divorce. Most often, pre-nups are associated with high net-worth individuals such as celebrity couples. However, a pre-nuptial agreement can be made by any couple without limitation to assets or financial status.

Although associated with love and romance, marriages also create legal and business relationships for some couples. In these instances, a pre-nuptial agreement can be seen as an insurance policy in the event of a divorce.

For others, marriage is viewed as a religious union and the presence of a pre-nup is frowned upon and considered as testing God's intentions. Regardless of your belief, here are a few pros and cons to consider when discussing the option of a pre-nuptial agreement with your fiancé.

Pros of a Pre-nup:

- It is inexpensive to establish compared to the costs of divorce proceedings, meditation, and legal representation fees.
- It can preserve the inheritance rights of children and grandchildren from prior marriages.
- If you have your own business or professional practice, a premarital agreement can protect business interests to prevent division and loss of control in the event of a divorce.
- If one spouse has more debt than the other, a premarital agreement can protect the debt-free spouse from having to assume the obligations of the other.
- A premarital agreement can address more than just financial topics. It can also address actions to be taken in the case of infidelity, abuse, or substance addiction.

- A premarital agreement can limit the amount of spousal support that one spouse will have to pay the other upon divorce.
- It is also important to note that a pre-nuptial agreement can be modified throughout the marriage with the consent of both individuals.

Cons of a Pre-nup:

- Signing a pre-nuptial agreement may require you to give up your right to inherit some or all of your spouse's estate when they die.
- If you contribute to the continuing success and growth of your spouse's business or professional practice, you may not be entitled to a fair share if you agree otherwise in a premarital agreement.
- Starting a relationship with a contract that sets forth the particulars of what will happen upon death or divorce may be viewed as proof of a lack of trust.

Staying in Control of Your Money

At all stages of your life, you should be in control and involved with the management of your money. All too often, women concede control of financial decisions to their husbands and partners without shared accountability. This can lead to unfortunate circumstances resulting in the mismanagement of money, late or unpaid bills, and a hopeless dependency on another person for your financial security and wellbeing. In order to stay in control of your money, even when married, consider the following recommendations:

Talk Everything Out... Again and Again

Prior to becoming married or sharing finances, it is critical to have a series of conversations discussing your individual financial statuses, goals, and how you two will partner to ensure strong financial management in your household. You may need the assistance of a neutral third party such as a counselor or spiritual advisor.

Such discussions should include:

- What is your annual income?
- What is your credit score?
- What outstanding debts do you have?
- What are your top 5 monthly spending categories?
- What is your opinion on the use of debt and revolving credit?
- Do you cover monthly expenses for anyone other than yourself (children, a parent, a sibling)?
- What is your view on loaning money?
- Do you donate to charities? How often and how much?
- On average, how much money do you spend (on vacations, gifts, holidays, clothing, and your car)?
- How do you think expenses should be split?

Budget Often

Develop a written or electronic budget that assists you in visualizing monthly income and expenditures. Spend 3-4 months perfecting the budget and dedicating your income to defined categories. Do not forget that you should also be budgeting for savings! Set up online alerts and notifications for abnormal spending habits, low balances, and upcoming bills.

Establish Financial Accounts

If married or in a domestic partnership, consider establishing a joint account for agreed-upon household expenses, such as rent, groceries, and utilities. This account should not replace your personal checking account or emergency fund. Based on prior conversations, agree on how each of you will contribute to the account. Options for shared contribution include a 50/50 split of all expenses or defined percentage based on your income. For example, if you make $60,000 and your husband makes $40,000, you would agree to contribute and cover 60% of monthly household expenses. The remaining money should be allocated to savings and investing.

Think Twice Before Co-Signing on Debt

Co-signing always seems like a good idea until it isn't! Co-signing represents the legal process of taking financial accountability for an item, such as a car, or long-term debt, such as student loans. It is very tempting to show affection and loyalty by helping a significant other with a loan. Unless you are married, this is often not a good idea. You should be aware that when you co-sign on a loan, you will remain responsible for the loan until the debt is repaid. Whether you remain in the relationship or not, you are accepting liability, and you are placing your credit and financial stability at risk. If your significant other asks you to co-sign on a loan, it means that they do not possess the financial readiness and strength to manage the loan themselves. The bank and other creditors view them as a risk and you should too. Rather than agreeing to co-sign, encourage your significant other to purchase a lower cost item that they can afford without your assistance.

5 Reasons to Start Advanced Planning Now

You Have or Plan on Having Children

Having children is a blessing that brings along new responsibilities and considerations. As most parents grow their families, attention to advanced planning is placed on the back burner until children become adults and/or the family has acquired sizable assets. However, this is a mistake.

Advanced planning is also critical for the assignment of guardianship in order to designate by who and how your children will be raised and provided for in the event of your unexpected death.

Parents should name legal guardians for their children and indicate how monetary funds can be utilized to support the children.

For parents of children with special needs or disabilities, it is critical to have open communication with potential guardians and ensure that ongoing requirements such as medical & therapeutic treatments are planned for your child.

You Want a Say in Your Medical Decisions

Contrary to popular belief, advanced planning is not just about what happens to you and your assets after death. One of the most effective uses of advanced planning is to provide healthcare related instructions if you are unable to speak for yourself. The completion of a durable healthcare power of attorney and living will, also known as a medical advance directive, provides instructions for how you want your medical team to care for you.

If you had a medical emergency and were unable to make decisions for yourself:

- Would you want to be placed on a ventilator?
- Would you like to donate your organs for medical research?
- Who should make the decisions for your care?

These questions are real life dilemmas that can be managed by proper planning and communication. In addition to having your important medical legacy planning documents completed, be sure to notify your loved ones of where the documents are stored and communicate your wishes in advance to avoid surprises.

You Have a Blended Family

Blended families often bring about increased complexity and consideration when reviewing advanced planning needs. One of the biggest mistakes that individuals make is the failure to update legal documents such as wills, trusts, and beneficiaries after life-changing events, including divorce, remarriage, adoption, or spousal separation.

Failure to update documents and reassess the potential distribution of assets may result in certain individuals, such as ex-spouses and stepchildren, being legally entitled to your inheritance even if that is not your wish at the time of your death.

You Own a Business

Ownership of a business adds a layer of complexity when considering advanced planning. If your business does not have a transfer of ownership or succession plan, you need one soon. If you are a small business, sole proprietor, or "mom and pop" shop, it is of particular importance to determine if and how your business should continue if you are medically unable to continue your work.

Questions for consideration:

- Can your business survive without you?
- Can you begin training a family member or dependent about your business operations for potential transfer of ownership?
- Do your children have an interest or the skills needed to manage your business for you?
- Where should your business assets, such as accounts receivables and owned property, go in the event of your death?
- If you are a solopreneur, is your family or a trusted loved one aware of key business documents such as deeds, articles of incorporation, and financial information?

You Are Single with No Heirs

Being single and having no natural heirs or beneficiaries is not an automatic pass on advanced planning. If you have a life insurance policy or have acquired a home or other sizeable assets, legacy planning is still beneficial.

Consider the following scenarios:

- You committed your intent to donate money to your favorite charity, church, or alma mater after your death but never legally established a charitable giving pledge.
- You want to use your life insurance to cover college expenses for your nieces and nephews, but your insurance policy has no named beneficiaries listed.
- You have specific requests for your funeral that may include cremation, donation of your body to science, or burial in a family cemetery.

In the case of these situations, advanced planning will prove to be effective and allow you to have peace of mind knowing that your wishes and desires will be managed.

Financial Tips for College Bound Millennials

Use a budget

Whether you are paying for college yourself, on scholarship, or receiving support from family members, it is advantageous to utilize a budget. Establish spending categories for fixed and variable expenses and consider online budgeting tools to hold yourself accountable.

Keep debt and credit cards to a minimum

It can be very tempting to sign up for your first credit card when you get on campus and are promised free swag and promotions. However, those credit card companies are banking on you to miss payments and overspend. Do not fall for the trap. Racking up credit cards is one of the biggest mistakes and can cost you thousands of dollars in interest payments and late fees. If you are already relying on student loans, remember that within 6 months of graduating, you will be responsible for paying those off too. Your best bet is to save money and use a debit card to keep risks low.

Rent your textbooks

Unless you are going to need your textbooks for more than 2-3 semesters, it is advantageous to rent your books. Look for deals online and outside of your student bookstore for the greatest savings.

Take advantage of student perks

Sign up for and use student discounts pertaining to food, transportation, free banking accounts, and travel.

Be responsible with refunds from scholarships and other sources

Refund checks are not free money. Use the funds to pay off any outstanding student loans or save the money for future needs.

Champagne Life on a Beer Budget

Have you ever been invited to an event or party and noticed those individuals who never eat or drink and have an excuse for why they need to leave early? Well, one obvious reason is the menu price! If you ever find yourself in unable to afford your meal, do not panic. Follow the steps below to enjoy the night and remain a gracious and classy guest.

1. When opening the menu and you see a $35 appetizer, remain calm.
2. Never express disgust or outrage regarding the menu pricing.
3. When the waiter comes to your table, ask him about any specials for the evening. You may find that some of the plates are discounted or that the restaurant has a *prix fixe* menu.
4. If a close friend is seated next to you at the table, feel free to state, "Gosh, everything looks so wonderful. Would anyone be interested in sharing something with me?"
5. Last and certainly not least, order a drink and nurse it throughout the night.

6. YOUR APPEARANCE

When it comes to millennial women and appearances, the hard truth is that you will be judged. No matter how elaborate your resume may be, no matter how many "connections" you have, or how affluent you are, your outward appearance and how you carry yourself will speak volumes. As such, it is important to realize and appreciate the power of your personal appearance and how it should be utilized to communicate your value and self-worth.

A millennial woman's personal appearance can take shape in many forms: wardrobe, hair care, skin care, and inner self. The next few pages of this chapter will focus on tips and suggestions that will enhance your outward and inner presence in order to ensure you always put your best foot forward.

- The Value of Self-Awareness
- 5 Tips to Make a Lasting First Impression
- Clothing Essentials
- Capsule Wardrobe
- Clothing Terminology 101
- Essential Jewelry 101
- Hair Care 101
- 10 Things to Always Have in Your Purse
- Handling Clothing Mishaps with Ease

The Value of Self-Awareness

A significant but underrated attribute of successful women is self-awareness. The ability to be aware of how you are perceived, valued, and viewed by others is critical in navigating business and personal relationships. Possessing self-awareness is like having an internal barometer enabling you to sense and adjust your behavior, conversation, physical appearance, and interactions with others.

The ability to gauge self-awareness can take place in many forms including:

Physical

- Do you double-check your clothing, grooming, and external presentation to ensure you are dressed well and putting your best foot forward?
- Are you aware of your body language, hand gestures, and physical stances when speaking with others?
- When speaking, are you aware of excess fidgeting, the occurrence of vocal fry, voice flight, and other habits that may be off-putting?

Professional

- Do you have a sense of how co-workers or classmates view and describe you?
- Is your work output regarded, sought after, and valued amongst your colleagues?
- Do you have professional or technical weaknesses that keep you from performing your best?
- Do you possess fears, insecurities, or other feelings that

prevent you from forming strong relationships and networking?
- Are you aware of your professional strengths and utilize them for success?

Social

- Are you mindful of the company you keep and how others may perceive them?
- Do you ensure your topics of conversation are non-offensive and acceptable in all social settings?
- Are you mindful of the content of your social media profiles?

5 Quick Tips to Make a Lasting First Impression

1. Get your clothes professionally tailored
2. Wear defining accessories
3. Possess a signature hairstyle
4. Always have a welcoming facial expression
5. Talk, think, and stand with confidence

Clothing Essentials

When it comes to dressing well, less can often be more. With so many shopping and e-commerce options, it can be tempting to always buy the latest trends. If you choose to do this, you may often find yourself short on cash or with a closet wardrobe that is expansive yet not functional. Instead, focus on making sure that you have a few pieces of essential clothing that can carry you at almost any state in your life.

Pants

- Tailored black trousers
- Opaque black leggings
- Dark wash denim jeans

Skirts

- Non-clingy pencil skirt

Dresses

- Knee level little black dress
- Cotton sundress
- One long, solid colored dress that can be used for dressy occasions

Shirts

- Crisp white dress shirt
- Basic black, white, and gray cotton tees
- Black turtleneck
- Well-fitted cardigan

Other

- Tailored black or navy suit
- Solid colored camisoles
- Neutral colored duster jacket

Accessories

- Ballet flats
- Riding boots
- Wedges
- Statement necklace
- Small pearl or gold earrings
- Neutral colored scarf

Capsule Wardrobe

A long-standing staple across the fashion industry is a capsule wardrobe. This concept represents the process of narrowing down your wardrobe to a minimal number of color palette aligned pieces that can be interchanged to make multiple outfits for casual and business wear.

Famous people known for the capsule wardrobe include Mark Zuckerberg and Steve Jobs. They wore the same brand and color of t-shirt and jeans no matter what. The capsule wardrobe is also revered by women in the corporate setting, frequent business travelers, or individuals who seem to spend countless hours fussing over what they should wear each day.

The capsule wardrobe represents your favorite, well-fitted clothes that can effortlessly be layered, interchanged, and combined to make multiple outfits.

Here are a couple of tips for getting your capsule wardrobe started.

Assign Clothes into Four Categories

1. Keep
You have worn this piece of clothing in the last 6 months and love the way it makes you feel.

2. Keep but out of season
You wear this clothing often, but it is now out of season.

3. Consider
You have not worn this piece of clothing in the last 6 months.

4. Discard/Donate
You have not worn this piece of clothing in the last 12 months.

Narrow Down

Once you have segmented down your clothing, focus on the keep pile.

Break down your keep pile into clothing types such as pants, skirts, dresses, top, and casual versus work looks. After separating by clothing type, look for similarities in color palates or material. Once you have segmented to a streamlined panel (for most people this includes beige, white, black, navy, gray, & denim), start creating interchangeable outfits.

Keep it simple

Many people who follow the capsule wardrobe strategy have less than 20 pieces of clothing in their capsule. Recognizing that this may be a stretch, you may want to start by creating a capsule per season.

Clothing Terminology 101

Below are the major dress code terms you should learn and stick to.

Casual

Can also be called "informal." Casual does not give you a pass to be sloppy and frumpy. You should still be tasteful and avoid worn-out clothing with holes, tears, and stains.

Smart casual

This can also be called "chic casual" or "dressy casual." You should aim for dressed-up versions of casual looks. For women, the same thing, but a nice knee-length skirt is acceptable as well. Depending on the setting, a pair of tailored jeans with a blazer can also be worn. It is best to avoid short-shorts, dated jeans, or t-shirts.

Business casual

Business casual can change depending on your age, work environment, and geographic location. Women should consider a skirt or dress with a hem past the knee, or tailored dress pants with a button-down or blouse.

Garden attire or beach formal

This means "dress to impress," but consider the environment when selecting your outfit. If it is "beach formal," sandals and other open-toe style shoes are acceptable. For "garden attire," wedge heels or flats are very appropriate and reduce your chances of sinking in the dirt or grass.

Resort wear

Resort wear is similar to garden/beach formal. Women often wear loose-fitting clothing such as summer dresses, palazzo pants, and colorful skirts.

Cocktail attire

Cocktail attire is a step above resort wear and offers you the opportunity to express yourself in loose or form-fitting attire. Darker colored clothing is popular at cocktail parties with women wearing knee-length skirts, dresses, or dress pants with a fitted blouse, or the classic "little black cocktail dress."

Festive

Festive is self-explanatory! Most often, you will wear festive wear during the months of Oct-Jan. This is the go-to dress code for holiday parties, New Year's Eve parties, and other themed get-togethers. Festive attire allows you to wear everything from sequins to furs!

Business formal

You will find this dress code for business lunches or conferences. Women should wear a tailored dress or pantsuit.

Semi-formal

This one can be a little tricky because it's a step below "black tie optional." Women can wear a little black cocktail dress, long dress, or a well-fitted pant suit. Dress shoes are expected, and a nice clutch should accompany your wardrobe.

Black tie optional

This is interchangeable with "formal attire." For women, a dress or pantsuit in a dark, neutral tone is acceptable. Even a cocktail-length dress is fine as long as it is not too colorful or flashy.

Black tie

This is considered the second highest level of formal attire. This is often the dress code to follow for evening weddings.

White tie

Can also be called "ultra-formal" because this is considered the highest level of dress code. Women should wear long, formal evening gowns, and gloves when enjoying cocktails.

Essential Jewelry 101

Jewelry can turn an outfit from good to great and give you an extra polished look.

Below are staple pieces that every millennial woman should have.

Watch for business or formal events
For maximum use and versatility, choose one with combined gold and silver tones.

Everyday watch
Show your personality by selecting a unique item, such as an oversized watch, fun colors, material, and/or cool functionality.

Travel watch
Reduce the worry when traveling by having a watch reserved for travel only. For under $10 a basic watch will do.

Stud earrings
White pearls, gold balls, diamond/cubic zirconia squares.

Hoop earrings
Gold and silver will pair well with an outfit. Be mindful of the hoop size, as less is more.

Formal drop earrings
For special evenings, have a nice pair of sparkly drop earrings on hand. Do not splurge on these. For under $50, you can find a solid costume pair at any department or beauty supply store.

Chain bracelet

To pull your look together, consider a nice chain-link bracelet in gold or silver.

Faux diamond

For dressy occasions, pick up a CZ studded bracelet for a dazzling effect.

Statement necklace

The perfect statement necklace has the ability to standalone and be the one item that can transform your outfit. Focus on having a statement necklace that is either bold in color, captivating in its design, or dazzling with jewels and gems. For statement necklaces to be effective, pair them with solid clothing and minimal additional accessories.

Sentimental piece

A piece of jewelry that brings positive memories to you due to where you acquired it, who gave it to you, or if it was owned by a dear loved one.

Hair Care 101

A great hairstyle can stand alone and offer you the confidence and extra boost of esteem whether you are in the classroom or boardroom. To ensure that your hairstyle looks great no matter your hair texture or length, consider the following healthy hair tips.

Washing

- Depending on your hair type, wash your hair at least once every 1 to 2 weeks.
- Hair should be washed to remove product build up while adding conditioner to maintain moisture and protection.
- Avoid products containing silicone, parabens, and sulfates. The products leave build-up and cause weak, limp, and unmanageable hair.

Styling

- Avoid styling techniques that involve applying excess heat to your hair.
- If using a blow dryer or curling iron, use a lower temperature setting and use a heat protectant spray. Remember, a flattening iron of 350-400 degrees puts off the same amount of heat needed to bake chicken. Should your hair be exposed to that much heat?
- Use detangler and other products and techniques that help reduce hair breakage and shedding.
- Use non-heat alternatives such as spiral rods, pin curls, twists, and loose braids to provide temporary texture and curl patterns.

Hair Styles

- Avoid tension-creating hairstyles for extended periods of time. Tight ponytails or tight braids can look chic, but they also put a lot of stress on your hair and scalp. Over time, this can create crimps and breakage in hair and stress the hair follicles, causing hairline thinning.
- Avoid using rubber bands and other elastic products in your hair, as they can cause tears and breakage. Instead, use a non-metal ponytail holder or clip.

Protective Hairstyles

Protective hairstyles are those that minimize the use of heat and excess styling. Protective hairstyles are great for improving the health of your hair.

- Protective hairstyles include: fishtail braids, cornrows, some hair extensions, clip-ins, and loose braids.
- Note that protective styles such as braids, cornrows, and weaves should not hurt. Excessive use of these styles may result in hair breakage, balding spots, and hair thinning.

Night Time Care

- Sleep on a satin or silk pillowcase to prevent frizz, breakage, and dryness. Cotton pillowcases tend to snag hair and create tiny rips and tears. They also tend to remove moisture from your hair, which can make it even more frizzy and brittle.
- Satin or silk pillowcases are also great for skin, as they do not draw out moisture the way cotton pillowcases do.

Extensions, Clip-Ons, and More

- If you want to add some quick length to your hair, choose sewn-in or clip-in weaves over glued-in weaves. Sew-ins or clip-ins are preferred over glued-in in order to protect your natural hair from heat damage and outdoor elements. Glued-in weaves can rip out your natural hair upon removal and contain non-natural chemical adhesives.
- Aim to have your weaves, braids, and extensions washed every 2-3 weeks to ensure the healthiness of your scalp.
- If you have coarse hair, moisturize your scalp with a lightweight oil or cream to reduce dryness and breakage around your edges.
- Monitor your hair weave to make sure it is not damp or wet for a prolonged period of time. Damp hair can lead to mildew, unpleasant smells, and an irritated scalp.
- When removing your braids, weaves, or clip-ins, let your natural hair rest for a few weeks by washing and conditioning it and holding off on heat-intensive styles.

10 Things to Always Have in Your Purse

1. At least $20 of cash in small bills
2. Cell phone charger
3. Personal identification
4. Pen and paper
5. Gum/Mints
6. Tissues
7. An item for protection (e.g. whistle, mace)
8. Feminine care products
9. Hair tie or bobby pins
10. Emergency contact information

Handling Clothing Mishaps with Ease

Let's face it, we have all had a clothing malfunction or two that ruins our entire day. Whether a run in your pantyhose, lipstick on your new white blouse, or an unexpected stain from a heavy cycle, clothing mishaps are always inconvenient and disruptive.

Stay prepared by considering the following:

- **Keep a scarf nearby**. A neutral colored pashmina (white, beige, black, or gray) can come in handy when you need to cover up an armpit stain, ketchup blot, or any other mishap that may occur above the waist.
- When traveling or during a day of important meetings and interviews, **wear dark colored clothing to hide accidental stains or spills**.
- **Keep a bottle of clear fingernail polish close by**. If you have ever suffered a run in your pantyhose, you understand that it is only a matter of time before the rip spreads like wildfire. A dab of clear fingernail polish can help hold the run and buy you time until your next important meeting. Dab clear polish on the area where the run occurred and let it dry. Note: clear polish can also be applied to costume jewelry and prevent your favorite "gold" ring from turning green!
- **Make a dryer sheet your friend!** In addition to helping remove static from clothing, dryer sheets can help keep stale clothes smelling fresh when in your suitcase or gym bag. If you travel often, consider always carrying a few dryer sheets with you. Not only will your clothes be fresh, but you can also swipe your clothing with the sheet and remove unwanted lint.
- If you have an office or locker at your place of work or school, never second-guess the importance of **keeping an**

extra set of clothes handy. Consider a basic black dress that can be great for a casual event or dressed up with the assistance of a scarf! It is also not a bad idea to have a basic pair of black pumps or flats on hand.
- **Use an absorptive substance such as baby powder to handle an oil stain.** Our immediate reaction is to blot stains with a napkin. This action often further entrenches the oil stain, making it larger and more difficult to remove. Instead, sprinkle powder on the stain and allow it to soak up the oil. After 2-3 minutes, place two fingers near the stain and pinch and pull your clothing. Release to make the excess powder fall away. Repeat until the stain is gone.
- **Keep a small sewing kit in your purse, glove compartment, or backpack.** This will come in quite handy in the unexpected event of a popped button or broken zipper.

7. MADAME MILLENNIAL ETIQUETTE

The previous chapter focused on personal appearance and the importance of demonstrating your worth through self-awareness and physical attributes. While your appearance may be your first impression, your on-going character, behaviors, and interactions with others maintain your reputation. Good etiquette is a universal language that will serve you well whether in the workplace or at home. Make an effort to ensure that you have a strong toolbox of etiquette best practices, ranging from being a good tipper to knowing the rules of unspoken communication. The following pages in this chapter will cover:

- 10 Commandments of Workplace Communication
- 10 Ways You are Unknowingly Offensive
- How to Start (and Hold) Great Conversations
- Responding to a Question When You Do Not Know the Answer
- The Importance of Timeliness
- The Rules for RSVP'ing
- Email 101
- Telephone 101
- Stationary 101

- Headphone Etiquette
- Mastering Unspoken Communication
- Alcohol Dos and Don'ts
- 20 Restaurant Words to Master

10 Commandments of Work Place Communication

Communicating within the workplace is an art. With multiple methods of communication, including email, phone, chat messenger, face-to-face interactions, and memos, it is challenging to ensure that you are communicating in the right manner with your team members.

Consider the following to ensure that your voice is heard and to protect yourself from workplace gossip and negative perceptions.

1. When having a meeting, demonstrate respect for the conversation by removing your cell phone from the table. Place it in your lap or purse.
2. When attending meetings, show your interest in the discussion by keeping your laptop closed or screen tilted down unless you are taking notes or presenting.
3. Aim to respond to client and colleague emails within 24 hours. If your response could take longer, reply to the sender, acknowledge their email, and inform them of the expected response time.
4. If you work in a shared office space or cubicle, be mindful of your conversations with others and while on the phone. For private or personal conversations, find a quiet space separate from your desk.
5. Be conscious of your use of hand gestures. Hand gestures should be used to add emphasis or expression to your conversation and sparingly in professional settings.
6. Never, ever, ever use workplace email or chat messages for negative or derogatory comments and discussions. Refrain from gossiping during meetings and over instant messen-

ger, or sending emails depicting co-workers or clients in a negative manner. This communication can be retrieved (even when deleted) and used against you or forwarded without your knowledge.
7. Refrain from placing email addresses in the "to" field until you have typed your message and proofread twice. This will eliminate emails sent by accident.
8. To convey important and time sensitive information, utilize multiple avenues of communication, including email, phone, and face-to-face discussions. Do not assume your recipient will act on your request from an email alone.
9. Aim to deliver bad information in person. Whether a poor performance review, the loss of a major client, or termination of an employee, in person communication is beneficial in conveying empathy, trust, and understanding.
10. Working remotely or from home through conference calls or video conference still requires professional communication. Establish a home office or quiet space for taking calls. Reduce background noise including dogs, children, and sirens. Ensure your communication equipment (webcam, headphones, and landline) are reliable. If using a webcam, be mindful of your appearance and dress according to your office dress code for virtual meetings.

10 Ways You Are Unknowingly Offensive

1. You are often late to events.
2. You do not follow-up with a thank you note or acknowledgment for gifts given to you or your children.
3. You bring uninvited guests with you to meetings or events.
4. You do not respect other people's time.
5. Your perfume is overwhelming or your make-up is excessive.
6. You associate with people that do not bring out the best in you.
7. You are often unreachable and do not respond to voicemails or text messages.
8. You are easily distracted and fail to follow-up on tasks and requests.
9. You ask for help but do not reciprocate favors.
10. You are often in a state of panic and appear to be frazzled and distressed.

How to Start (and Hold) Great Conversations

The ability to navigate a social setting is not that difficult to develop. What is critically challenging is laying the foundation for strategic personal and professional relationships within only a few seconds. This act requires you to gain the attention of another person but also to leave them wanting to have a future conversation with you!

Some of you are natural-born talkers! You can walk into a room, metro station, restaurant, or any office and strike up a great conversation. For others, the thought of speaking to someone other than your closest friend makes you shiver.

Regardless of your comfort level, keep this handy tool in your back pocket: the A to Z Game.

Before you attend an event, prepare by having a brief topic to discuss that corresponds with each letter of the alphabet. Here are a few topics to consider; however, your list should be based on current events, the purpose of the event you are attending, or the individual that you are meeting with.

Example:
A-American Politics
B- Business News
C-Career Background
F-Financial Market
M-March Madness
T-Travel Experiences

Responding to a Question When You Do Not Know the Answer

One of the most awkward situations occurs when you are in the middle of a conversation, and someone asks you a question for which you do not have an answer.

The level of embarrassment may vary depending on who or how many people you are speaking with. Regardless, keeping your cool can make all the difference.

1. **Pause.** This buys you time to think of an answer or to let someone answer on your behalf.
2. **Keep your composure** and state, "That's an insightful question. Tell me more about what leads you to ask that." Not only have you bought yourself more time, but you have also forced the person you are speaking with to restate their question in a more thoughtful manner and to give you more support in answering.
3. **Do not lie** and never try to fake your way into an answer.
4. **Acknowledge and pivot.** Continue the conversation. If the question intrigues you, feel comfortable stating, "That's a question I haven't fully considered and will have to give more thought to." After stating this, smile, and pivot to another conversation or discussion point that you feel more comfortable with.

The Importance of Timeliness

Picture this: you and your college best friend are planning to catch up at 11 AM over coffee. You have taken an extended work break and are looking forward to downloading all the latest news. As you settle into your cozy spot at the coffee shop, you look at the clock—11:05 AM. Your phone vibrates with a text from your friend: "Hey girl, running late! Should be there in about 20 min. xoxo." What do you do?

We have all been in situations where we are either running behind schedule or waiting on someone who is late.

While life happens, here are a couple of suggestions for managing timeliness.

If you are running late

- Notify your party as soon as you recognize that you are behind schedule, NOT at the time you were planning to meet.
- Give your party the option to reschedule. For example, if you are 15 minutes behind for a 30-minute coffee break, call the person, apologize about your tardiness, and ask if it is better to reschedule based on their availability.
- Once you arrive, apologize for your tardiness!
- Offer to pick up an extra portion of the bill, drink, or appetizer.
- For future appointments, give yourself more time to prevent reoccurring lateness.

If you are waiting for someone

- Determine how long you can wait without interfering

with your subsequent plans. (This shows that you value and respect your own time.)
- If your guest has not arrived on time, call or send a message asking about their expected time of arrival.
- If the waiting time is acceptable, wait.
- If not, inform your guest that you need to cut your meeting short or reschedule.
- Never feel bad about having to reschedule due to someone else's tardiness.

The Rules for RSVP-ing

Beginning in the spring each year, millennial women are inundated with invitations for everything from birthday parties and bridal showers to graduations and weddings. If you are a social butterfly, you may find yourself with more invitations than you can handle. Not only does this place a potential strain on your time, it also can be stressful to your budget.

Although RSVP is the French abbreviation for répondez s'il vous plaît (response please), it should mean respect please! Even though you do not have to attend all invited events, you should show respect to the person who invited you by following these steps.

Make a timely decision

Soon after receiving your invitation, make an appropriate decision on whether or not you will be able to attend the event. Refrain from waiting until the last minute to send your response.

Respond in the same manner that you were invited

General etiquette calls for you to respond to the invitation in the same manner that you received it. If you are short on time or need to change your attendee response, it is best to contact the host or person who invited you to send your regrets.

Keep Your Response Brief if You Cannot Attend

Although not required, it is common courtesy to provide a brief explanation for why you cannot attend the event. Do not lie about your reason and keep it to a minimum, such as "I will be out of town," or "I have a prior commitment on this date."

Follow-Up with a Gift or Congratulatory Note

Not attending an event does not excuse you from your obligation to acknowledge the event with a note of congratulations or a gift. The general rule of thumb is to follow-up with the same type of gift or acknowledgment you would have given had you attended in person.

Changing Your Mind

If for some reason you are able to attend the event after declining, it is important to get the approval of the host first. Under many circumstances, the host has a set number of individuals they invited for planning purposes. Do not be rude by showing up without prior notice and do not bring any uninvited guests with you.

Email 101

Email is the dominant method of communication in the workplace and in most people's personal lives. As such, it is important to know proper email etiquette and tips to keep your email game strong!

1. Always have a separate work and personal email account. Privacy is no longer a right. It is important that you separate your personal communication and messages from those of your work life.
2. Give careful thought to the name and domain of your personal email address.
3. Personal does not mean casual. Your email address should only reflect an aspect of your name or business. Email names such as littlecutie@123.com or #1baby@234.com make a statement about your character and ability to self-reflect. Additional consideration should be given to excluding personal email addresses that identify your race, political affiliation, or religious beliefs.
4. Your email signature is not the place to list a mini resume or to convey personal thoughts.
5. Be mindful of the content of your emails. You should never send email messages that speak disdainfully of another person or implicate you in wrongdoing. If you would not feel comfortable with the emails being read aloud in a staff meeting, then you should refrain from sending.
6. Prevent accidental submissions of draft emails. When replying to emails remove the email address of the sender until you have finished typing and proofread your message.
7. Never send emails that discuss an individual, offer "top secret" information, or include thoughts of sabotage and

revenge. Regardless of how computer savvy you may be, there is always a way to retrieve your emails and deleted messages. It is best to always think twice about the content, tone of voice, and information in an email.

8. Communicate your bottom line early in your email. Channel your inner solider and communicate the bottom line up front. Keep your email messages brief and to the point. Start each message with the key reason or purpose for writing.

Telephone 101

Answering the Phone

How you answer the phone often depends on the caller. However, if you do not recognize a number, answer the phone in a consistent and professional manner. A standard answering phrase could be "Andrea speaking" or "This is Naomi."

Recording a Voicemail Greeting

The quality and content of your voicemail messages is paramount. When recording your voicemail message, consider the following:

- Record the message in a location that is free of background noise
- State your full name
- Instruct the caller to leave only necessary information

Example: "You have reached the voicemail of Marie St. Clair. I apologize for missing your call. Please leave your name, number, and a brief message, and I will return your call at my earliest convenience."

Leaving a Voicemail

Also important is how you leave a voicemail for a co-worker or friend. The clarity and intent of your message can make a difference in the timeliness of the response you receive. Simply stating, "Call me back," is ineffective.

Friendly Voicemail: "Hi, Jim! This is Marie. I am calling to follow up on our discussion from last week. Please call me at your earliest convenience."

Urgent Voicemail: "Hi, Jim! This is Marie St. Clair from Purchasing. I am calling to finalize the details of next week's retreat. Due to our tight deadline, I would like to have your comments on a few items. Please give me a call at 555-555-5555. I will be in the office until 4:30 this afternoon."

Mandatory Callback: "Jim—this is Marie St. Clair. It seems that we are playing phone tag, but due to the urgency in our timeline, it is important that we touch base today. I need your comments on 1) pricing for the staff retreat, 2) transportation options, and 3) existing corporate sponsors. You can reach me at 555-555-5555 until 4:30 today. After this time, please call me on my cell at 552-555-5555 or via email at Mstclair@123.com."

Public Cell Phone Use

Cellular phones are a necessary part of how millennials conduct business and maintain personal relationships. Although cell phones provide immediate access to communication and convenience, there are certain situations where cellphone use should be avoided. This includes:

- When you are using the bathroom.
- When receiving customer service. Please refrain from walking up to a counter, drive-thru, bank teller, or reception desk while on the phone.
- In a small space such as a doctor's waiting room, nail salon, or hotel elevator.

If any of these situations are unavoidable and you must use your phone, do the following: apologize to those around you, lower your voice, and move to a more private location to resume your call.

Cell Phone Ringtones

It is time to put an end to eccentric and customized ringtones such as songs, inspirational speeches, and lively/pop tunes. Keep it classy with a basic ringtone you can recognize or keep your phone on vibrate.

Stationery

The use of stationery is a way to communicate your feelings of appreciation, admiration, and most importantly…class.

In our society, it is very easy to send a quick email or instant message. However, taking the time to write a simple thank you note speaks volumes about your personality and character.

Stationery is most beneficial in the following circumstances:

- After receiving a gift
- After meeting a new professional networking contact you want to keep in touch with. (Always include a business card.)
- When you want to expresses thoughts of congratulations, sympathy, or apologies Consider taking your class up a notch by ordering personalized stationery from an online distributor or local store. Custom design your stationery to highlight your personality and flare!

Headphone Etiquette

Headphones have become all too popular and are even regarded as fashionable accessories.

Headphones give you the ability to cancel out the rest of the world when you are on a bus or flight with a screaming baby. In such circumstances, it is fine to crank up the volume (to a respectable level) and release some daily stress.

However, there are occasions and locations where headphones should be avoided. This includes:

- Your workplace—Even if you work in a cubicle, wearing earphones can make you come off as distant, unapproachable, and reclusive
- Places of worship
- While driving
- When conducting a transaction such as visiting an ATM teller, ordering food, or picking up clothes from the cleaners

Note that some environments, including workplaces, will have a company culture that is accepting of behaviors such as wearing earphones. As a rule of thumb, ask your boss or co-worker about the appropriate protocol before you partake.

Mastering Unspoken Communication

Unspoken communication, including body language and facial expressions, often has the ability to convey stronger messages than actual words. The ability to read someone else's body language can be very beneficial in your personal and professional life. It is critical to have self-awareness about your own body language, posture, and facial expressions when around others. Many women are often assumed to be upset, mad, or disinterested in conversation due to their facial expressions.

Learning to be aware of your expressions and body language can be used to your advantage in the following situations:

- When you are negotiation a job offer or salary
- When you have heard information that will give you a competitive advantage at work
- When you hear contradictory information from a boss or co-worker
- When someone gives a snide remark about you or your acquaintances
- When you are accused of doing something wrong when you are innocent

For illustration, if you feel that you are being attacked by a co-worker or peer:

- Do not fold your arms.
- Instead, put your hands in your pockets or at your side, and stare into the person's eyes.
- Allow the individual to continue his or her rant.
- When he or she has finished, state, "I can tell that you are upset. I also need a moment and will follow up with you."
- Go to your desk, document what the person said, and

write the names of those individuals who witnessed the altercation.
- Allow yourself time to process the occurrence and gather any factual data that you may need to support your claim.
- Schedule an intervention/debriefing meeting with the individual and a third-party.
- In any situation, please consider your personal safety first.

Alcohol Dos and Don'ts

It's happy hour somewhere, right? For many of us, this phrase signals the time to wind down and enjoy the end of a hard workday. However, there may be several occasions when declining a drink will be in your best interest.

In the age of omnipresent social media, one's lifestyle can be shared via a quick tweet, post, or photo. As such, you never want to position yourself in a negative light and put your character at risk. Although it may seem harmless to take a quick selfie or other photo with friends, be cautious and ensure that you are never photographed with a drink in your hand (unless it is your wedding day)! One innocent photograph can be misconstrued and frame you in the wrong light.

To err on the side of caution, here are a few situations when declining an alcoholic beverage is in your best interest:

- You are "on the clock" and responsible for work-related duties (this includes during a lunch break)
- Attending a work-related event with senior leadership present
- Attending religious functions (except for communion, of course)
- Dating someone new. Stay empowered to make quick and smart decisions in case of an emergency or uncomfortable situation
- No one else is drinking
- You are being photographed
- You are responsible for someone else's child
- When you do not want to
- On long flights

Phrases to use when declining a drink include:

- "No, thank you. I have an early morning tomorrow."
- "Thanks for the offer, but I'm pacing myself."
- "Thank you, but no. Perhaps another time."
- "I'm fine right now, but I may take you up on it in a little bit."

If you work in an environment where social drinking is a rite of passage and you do not want to seem anti-social, just get a mocktail. For beer, consider O'Doul's, and for cocktails, cranberry juice or ginger ale with lime and straw will also do the trick!

20 Restaurant Words to Master

Al dente: cooked pasta, firm to the taste
A-la mode: with ice cream
A-la carte: individual food items that are priced separate from the entrée
Aioli: flavored mayonnaise
Au gratin: means cooked with butter and/or cream and topped with cheese or breadcrumbs
Baguette: classic long, thin loaf of bread
Bisque: a thick, rich soup often made with cream
Braised: to cook in fat and then stew
Caramelized: browned with heat and sugar
Carbonara: a sauce that includes cream, eggs, Parmesan cheese and bits of bacon
Compote: stewed fresh or dried fruit
Condiments: spices or sauces used to flavor food
Confit: meat salted and cooked in its own fat
Delicatessen: a deli
Foie-grais: luxury food made from duck or goose liver
French press: coffee pot with a plunger and built in filter
Gourmand: a person who is fond of food
Gourmet: culinary art of fine food
Halal: foods conforming to Islamic dietary laws
Hollandaise: a sauce made of butter, egg yolks, and lemon juice
Hors d'oeuvre: appetizers served before meals
Kosher: foods conforming to Jewish dietary laws
Maître d': head manager of a restaurant or small hotel
On the rocks: served over ice
Palate: a person's appreciation of taste and food
Panko fried: fried with light and crispy breadcrumbs

Prix Fixe: fixed price menu offering a short list of the restaurant's food selection

Rémoulade: a sauce made of mayonnaise and mustard, capers, gherkins, herbs, and anchovies

Roux: a mixture of flour and fat (butter, drippings or pork or beef fat) used to thicken mixtures, such as soups and sauces

Seared: food quickly browned at a high temperature

Sommelier: expert wine waiter

Sous chef: staff member who assists the main chef

Tempura: a Japanese version of batter-dipped and deep-fried

8. A BALANCED HOME

Of all the topics that this book covers, home life and your domestic happiness correlate the most to your overall well-being and ability to succeed as an employee, spouse, mother, and friend. If your home isn't happy, you are not happy. For many millennial women with or without children, juggling additional responsibilities, such as meal preparation, cleaning, caring for others, and functioning as the CEO of a household, can be tiresome and daunting.

Coincidentally, the physical state of your home (clothes piled up everywhere and dust on furniture) correlates with your stress levels at work or in your personal life. As a result, these responsibilities fall to the bottom of your priorities until you have the downtime to focus on them. One way to better manage responsibilities of the home is to implement systems, routines, and fail-proof methods that help you organize your home faster and more efficiently. The following pages of this chapter will cover:

- Gaining Efficiency in Your Life
- Ten Ways to Save Time During the Day
- Maximizing Your Grocery Shopping Experience
- Kitchen Must-Haves
- Fail-proof Recipes
- Fail-proof Home Cleaning Tips

- Spring Cleaning
- Bathroom Cabinet Essentials
- Junk Drawer Judy
- How Often Do I? Rules of the Home

Gaining Efficiency in Your Life

Whether for work, home, or elsewhere, developing systems and processes to help you manage the unpredictable is key to increasing efficiency and de-stressing your day-to-day life.

Greater efficiency is gained by limiting unexpected variability, pre-planning, and by having defined systems in place.

What is a system?

A system is a repeatable, reliable, and effective method for getting things done. The most common and recognizable systems take place in the workplace. This includes email management, regular staff meetings, quality assurance methodologies, and standard policies and procedures.

If you were to interview a supermom, a successful entrepreneur, or leadership of a top Fortune 500 company, one of the things that they would all have in common is that they have systems and processes in place that help them manage their schedules and overall quality of work life.

Here are the key areas where systems can provide great value in your personal life:

- Finances
- Wardrobe
- Meal preparation
- Personal relationships and children
- Stress management

In order to begin establishing systems, consider the following:

Identify what gives you the most stress

For example:

- Are you often running late?
- Does your manager overload you with requests and tasks?
- Are you constantly misplacing things?
- Do your clients demand your time but you are always delayed in your response and the ability to follow up?

Determine what 1-2 things you can change in order to reduce the stress.

For example:

- Can you reprogram your morning routine to get you out the door faster?
- Can you better upward manage your boss?
- Do you need to reduce clutter in your home?
- Can you rearrange your inbox to better prioritize important messages?

Start small

- Give yourself time to adjust to your new schedule
- Use reminders, accountability partners, and other tools to encourage adherence.

Ten Ways to Save Time During Your Day

1. **Cook bulk meals on the weekend.** Portion and freeze meals for lunch and dinner. Grab meals in the morning and have them available throughout the work week.
2. **Pack your gym bag the night before** to reduce excuses for not making it to the treadmill.
3. **Eliminate morning wardrobe indecisiveness** by having one or two go-to outfits. Dress up the outfit using scarves, statement jewelry, and other accessories.
4. **Read email and listen to voicemails before** going into your workplace.
5. **"Outsource" one aspect of your routine.** Consider home grocery delivery, laundry pickup and delivery service, dog walking, home lawn care, and child pickup.
6. **Prepare your breakfast the night before.** Have a coffee/tea cup ready and cereal or fresh fruit cut, prepared, and stored.
7. **Block off time on your own calendar** to limit workplace interruptions. Use the time to complete lingering tasks.
8. **Turn off email and phone notifications.** Unless you are awaiting a high priority email or message, turn off notifications. The constant alerts, pop-up messages, and noises can be more of a distraction and take you away from prioritized activities.
9. **Commit to saying no.** This sounds strange, but the endless requests from of others can zap your time and energy. Whether a request to attend an ad hoc meeting, take on another project, or bake an unexpected batch of cupcakes for your kid's classroom, learn to decline and feel great doing it.
10. **Master a hairstyle that makes you feel great** and requires little effort in the morning.

Maximizing Your Grocery Shopping Experience

The fastest way to run up a grocery bill is to go shopping while hungry and without a pre-planned list! Regular grocery shopping should consist of replenishment of staple foods and the purchasing of perishable items. If you often find yourself in the grocery store wandering and grabbing items off the shelf, your wallet (and your waistline) are paying for it.

Step 1
Make a standard grocery template of all the items that you and your family consume on a monthly basis.

Step 2
Using your grocery template, assess existing grocery items in your home.

Step 3
Based on recipes planned for the week, determine your grocery needs and budget for the week.

Step 4
Set a weekly schedule for grocery trips to limit unplanned visits.

Step 5
Go shopping with a plan. Recognize that the healthiest way to maneuver the grocery store is to "horseshoe" shop. If you think of most grocery stores, they are in the shape of a U or horseshoe. Most produce, meats, and fresh protein are on the perimeter and processed, higher carbohydrate, non-perishable foods are in the

aisles. Shopping primarily around the perimeter of the grocery store can support healthy and clean eating lifestyles.

Kitchen Must-Haves

Moving into a new place, looking to clean up your pantry, or finding yourself always struggling to come up with a great meal? Consider restocking your shelves with these kitchen must-haves. These ingredients are multi-purpose and are interchangeable in order to create an excellent meal.

Condiments

- Apple cider vinegar
- Balsamic vinegar
- BBQ sauce
- Ketchup
- Maple syrup
- Mayonnaise
- Mustard (Regular & Dijon)
- Peanut butter
- Salsa
- Soy sauce
- Teriyaki sauce
- Vinegar
- White wine vinegar
- Worcestershire sauce

Spices

- Allspice
- Bay leaves
- Cayenne pepper
- Cinnamon
- Cumin
- Ginger
- Ground pepper
- Honey
- Italian seasoning
- Kosher salt
- Onion powder
- Paprika
- Thyme
- Vanilla extract

Non-Perishables

- Beans
- Beef broth
- Bottled water
- Breadcrumbs
- Canned diced tomatoes
- Canned fruits
- Canned tuna fish
- Canned vegetables
- Cereal
- Chicken stock
- Coffee (instant and brewed)
- Cooking spray
- Cornstarch
- Crackers
- Oatmeal/grits
- Pancake batter
- Pasta/spaghetti noodles
- Peanut butter
- Rice
- Tea
- Tomato paste
- Tomato sauce

Perishables

- Cheese
- Bread
- Butter
- Eggs
- Fresh fruit
- Fresh vegetables
- Garlic
- Lemons
- Limes
- Milk
- Onions
- Protein source such as lean meat
- Yogurt

Fail-Proof Recipes

Whether you are cooking a regular nightly dinner, planning a special meal for a guest, or looking for an easy dish that you can share with a friend, you should always have a few signature dishes you can whip up with ease.

What follows are a few recipes that standalone or can be enhanced with a few additional ingredients.

Lemon Pepper Chicken

Basic Ingredients
Whole chicken
Freshly squeezed lemon juice
Kosher salt
Ground black pepper

Get Fancy by Adding
3-4 bay leaves
Chopped onions and celery
Thyme
Basil
Italian seasoning

Cooking Directions
Sprinkle chicken with spices.
Place ingredients in crock-pot.
Let it cook for 8-10 hrs.
Serve with rice or vegetables.

Pasta and Tomato Sauce

Basic Ingredients:
Pasta of your choice
Tomato sauce of your choice
Kosher salt
Ground black pepper
Garlic

Get Fancy by Adding
Ground turkey, ground beef, or Italian sausage
Chopped onions, green peppers, and mushrooms
Chili powder

Directions
Boil pasta.
Cut and then sauté vegetables in skillet.
Add protein to skillet and brown.
Add spices and seasoning.
Pour tomato sauce in skillet.
Separately drain water from pasta.
Mix pasta sauce and vegetables with drained pasta.
Serve.

Meatballs

Basic Ingredients

40 to 50 fully cooked, frozen meatballs
1 cup ketchup
1/2 cup grape jelly

Directions

Mix ingredients.
Simmer until meatballs are ready to eat.

Oven Roasted Sweet Potatoes

Basic Ingredients
3-4 Fresh sweet potatoes
Salt
Olive oil

Get Fancy by Adding
Fresh lemon juice

Directions
Wash potatoes with skin on and cut sweet potatoes into large bite size chunks.
Place cut potatoes in oven-safe dish.
Drizzle olive oil over potatoes.
Sprinkle salt over potatoes.
For a zesty finish, squeeze juice of 1/2 lemon.
Stir potatoes in dish to mix ingredients.
Cover with foil.
Place in oven at 345 degrees for 30-45 min or until brown.
Remove and serve.

Avocado Salad

Basic Ingredients
Avocado
Cucumbers
Roma tomatoes
Fresh lemon juice
Olive oil
Salt

Get fancy by adding
Chilled cooked shrimp
Yellow curry
Roasted red pepper flakes

Directions
Cut 2 cucumbers and 4 tomatoes into small bite-sized pieces.
Drizzle olive oil on top.
Sprinkle kosher salt on top.
Squeeze juice of 1/2 of lemon.
Stir ingredients in bowl.
Cut avocado in small bite-sized pieces.
Stir gently.
Serve within 2-3 hours to prevent avocado from browning or softening.

Kitchen Sink Breakfast Pie

Basic Ingredients

Eggs
Shredded cheese of your choice
1 frozen pie shell package
Kosher salt
Ground black pepper

Get Fancy by Adding

Ground meat, bacon, sausage, tofu, or shrimp
Spinach
Mushrooms
Chopped tomatoes
Peppers (Red or Green)
Chopped onions

Directions

Preheat oven to 350 degrees.
Mix all ingredients in bowl.
Pour ingredients into pie shell.
Sprinkle any remaining cheese on top.
Bake for 25 minutes or until firm.
Remove from oven and let sit for 15 min.
Cut and serve with fresh fruit.

Peach Cobbler

Basic Ingredients

2 32 oz. cans of sliced peaches—retain 1 cup of liquid
3 frozen pie shell packages (make sure each package has 2 pie shells)
1/4 cup of all-purpose flour
4 dashes of cinnamon
1/2 teaspoon Vanilla extract
2 dashes Allspice
3 dashes Nutmeg
1/2 stick of butter
Egg whites

Directions

Preheat oven to 350.
In a large skillet or saucepan, bring peaches and butter to a simmer.
By hand, sprinkle flour to thicken mix.
Reduce heat and add vanilla extract and all spices.
Set thickened mixture aside.
Place frozen pie shells in oven for 5 min to warm.
Remove pie shells from oven.
Take cobbler mixture and pour into pie shell.
Take other pie shell and use dough to cover the top of the mixture.
Place in oven for 25 minutes.
Remove from oven and brush egg whites on top of dough for glossy finish.
Place back in oven for 15 minutes.
Remove from oven and let it sit for 20 minutes.
Serve with vanilla ice cream.

Chocolate Peanut Clusters

Basic Ingredients
2 bags of chocolate (dark or milk)
1 32 oz. jar of peanuts

Get Fancy by Adding
Crushed peppermint as sprinkled topping

Directions
Cover large baking pan with parchment paper and set aside.
Add 3 cups of water to small saucer and bring water to a boil.
Create a double saucer by placing a second larger saucer on top of smaller saucer.
Pour chocolate into large saucer until chocolate melts.
If needed, add more water to smaller pot to ensure that water does not evaporate.
Once all chocolate has melted, pour in peanuts and stir.
Using tablespoon, place spoon-sized dollops of chocolate-peanut mix on parchment covered pan.
Place pan into freezer for 2-3 hours.
Remove and serve at room temperature.

Fail-proof Home Cleaning Tips

Let's face it! Home cleaning is one of those things that you either love or hate to do. Regardless of your stance, here are a few foolproof cleaning tips that will make sure your humble abode is spotless.

Kitchen

- Clean your microwave by placing a small bowl filled with water and lemon juice inside and warming for 1 min. Wipe clean with paper towel or sponge.
- Eliminate refrigerator odors by pouring ½ cup of white vinegar in a cup and placing it in the fridge for 1-3 hours.
- Place 3-4 extra trash bags in the bottom of your garbage can to have one on hand after taking out the trash.
- To get unwanted grime and burnt food off pans, add Ajax and water. Boil mixture in pan for 15 minutes and then remove stains.
- Hate the smell of old sponges? Rinse them with hot water and soap and then microwave them for 2 minutes, or throw them in your dishwasher during your next wash.
- Utilize crock-pot liners to reduce clean-up after cooking a savory dish.
- Keep a small bowl or cup of vinegar near your fruit bowl or sink to catch and eliminate fruit flies during warm months.

Bathroom

- Clean grout and other mold-prone areas using a homemade mixture of bleach and baking soda. Apply mixture

as a paste, allow to sit for 5 minutes, use an old toothbrush for stubborn spots, and wipe clean.
- Remove stains and soap scum from your tub using liquid toilet bowl cleaner. Spread well, let it sit for 10 minutes, wipe clean with a sponge, and then rinse.
- Eliminate toilet odor by adding ½ cup of bleach to the bowl. Let it sit for one hour and then flush. For an eco-friendly version, use white vinegar.
- Spray sink and bath faucets with bleach to reduce mildew and mold build up.

Laundry

- To remove the black gunk from your iron, generously sprinkle salt over a pillow case or towel. Iron the salt covered towel without steam; continue this process until black gunk is minimal. Wipe away excess residue.
- Clothes smell like mildew no matter the number of washes? It may be time to clean your washing machine. Remove mildew smells by running your washing machine with 2 cups of white vinegar and 2 cups of bleach alone. Run for a full cycle and voila!
- Spare the dust and lint nightmare by keeping a mini-trashcan in your laundry room. Use the can to dispose of dryer lint, dryer sheets, and other build up.

Spring Cleaning

Spring cleaning is the seasonal process of de-cluttering your home, updating your closet, and taking care of both external and internal domestic duties to keep your home updated and clean. Review the checklist below to make your spring-cleaning process easy and organized.

General Cleaning

- Remove longstanding areas of clutter.
- Check exterior of home for signs of rodent or bug infestations.
- Sweep or vacuum all areas.
- Check boxes and other storage items for signs of mold.
- Give away or discard any unwanted items.
- Shampoo carpets and rugs.
- Clean windows and window treatments.

Kitchen

- Remove everything from the refrigerator and freezer.
- Pull out shelves and bins to clean hard-to-reach places.
- If possible, move the fridge in order to clean underneath and wipe all sides.
- Assess food items that were stored in fridge and freezer. Discard old condiments and any freezer burned foods.
- Place a small cup of white wine vinegar in the fridge to neutralize odors.
- After an hour, place bins and shelves back in and organize the fridge.

Spice rack

- Re-organize your spice rack by removing all items.
- Use a wet paper towel or cloth to clean up spilled remnants of spices.
- Check spices for overall freshness.
- Discard old products and rearrange spice rack either alphabetically or by size.
- Consider purchasing a spice organizer or Lazy Susan for optimization of space.

Storage containers

- Identify and place all Tupperware and storage containers in a central location.
- Ensure that all items have matching lids and are free from cracks and unsightly stains.
- Discard or re-purpose mismatched pieces.

Pantry

- Perfect your pantry by completing a thorough assessment of non-perishable items.
- Ensure that all items are within their expiration date.
- Check pantry for any spills to reduce the risk of bugs/rodents.
- Donate any items not needed to a local food pantry.
- Re-organize items based on the frequency of use, alphabetically, or by size.

Bedroom

- Remove all bed sheets and mattress pads.

- Vacuum mattress and box springs.
- Remove all clutter from underneath the bed.
- Rotate bed and change blankets.
- Turn over your mattress to distribute pressure points.
- Replace cool-weather bedding with warm-weather bedding.
- Replace or wash pillows with washing machine to eliminate mold and bacteria.
- Place lavender sachets under your mattress pad or sheets to enjoy a calming sleep each night.

Bathroom

- Wash all bathroom rugs and sanitize floors.
- Deep clean shower, tub, sink bowls, and toilet.
- Conduct an inventory of beauty products and toiletries.
- Discard any expired or discolored products.
- Wash make-up brushes and make-up bags.
- Review and dispose any expired medicine cabinet items and prescriptions.

Closet Organization

- Try on clothing to ensure proper fit.
- Remove any clothing that is out of season or no longer fits.
- Store out-of-season clothing in garment bags or storage cubes.
- Donate apparel you no longer wear.
- Organize your closet by clothing type and color.
- Add cedar blocks or other air fresheners to keep moths and odors away.

Living Room

- Deep clean fabric-covered furniture and upholstery.
- Shampoo carpets and rugs, and deep clean and sanitize hardwood or tile flooring.
- Dust around all baseboards, windows, and blinds.
- Remove and professionally clean fabric window treatments.
- Clean window glass and doors.
- Dust and clean air vents, fireplace mantel, TVs, and décor such as picture frames and books.
- Place air fresheners and deodorizers to keep your home smelling fresh.

Office Organization

- Review all paper files and organize by type (e.g., bills, insurance policies, taxes).
- Determine which files should be digitized or destroyed.
- Electronically organize, back up, and delete unneeded computer files.
- Assess electronics and other gadgets.
- Organize chargers, wires, and sell or donate idle equipment.

Outdoor Cleaning

- Clean porch ceilings and walls.
- Sweep up cobwebs and debris.
- Wash walls with all-purpose cleaner.
- Inspect light fixtures and replace non-working light bulbs.

Bathroom Cabinet Essentials

Before you make another splurge trip to your local pharmacy or department store, make sure you are aware of essential items for a well-stocked bathroom.

- Ace bandage
- Anti-diarrheal
- Antibacterial cream
- Antifungal cream
- Antihistamines
- Aspirin
- Band-Aids
- Bug spray
- Cotton balls
- Cough medicine
- Decongestant
- Diuretic
- Extra pair of glasses or contacts
- Eyeglass repair kit
- Feminine products
- Gauze
- Heating pad
- Hydrogen peroxide
- Ibuprofen
- Laxatives
- Medical tape
- Needle and thread
- Neosporin
- Q-tips
- Rubbing alcohol
- Saline drops
- Sleep medication

- Sunscreen
- Thermometer
- Throat lozenges
- Tweezers

Junk Drawer Judy

One place in the house that often contains the most clutter is the junk drawer. In theory, a "junk drawer" should be a "utility drawer," functioning as a central and organized place that contains common but valuable items.

Here is a list of common junk drawer items that can make your life a bit easier:

- Batteries
- Blank envelopes
- Clear and duct tape
- Emergency candles
- Emergency contact phone numbers
- X-Acto knife
- Extra chargers
- Extra $20 in multiple bill forms
- Eyeglass repair kit
- Safety pins/thumbtacks
- Scissors
- Screwdrivers
- Set of matches/lighter
- Sewing kit
- Spare house/car key
- Stamps

How Often Do I? Rules of the Home

Change home air filters
Every 3 months

Change my bed sheets
Every 7-10 days

Clean my shower or bath tub
After each use: deep clean biweekly

Clean my carpet
Every 3-6 months

Clean my oven
Every 3 months

Keep frozen food
Depends on the food but often, no more than 3 months

Change my car oil
Every 3 months or 3000-5000 miles

Put air in my tires
Depends on your driving habits, but you should check air levels every month and before road trips

Keep kitchen sponges
No more than 30 days

Flip my mattress
Every 3 months

Clean my mattress
Every 3 months by vacuuming

Clean my purse
At least weekly

Wash my pillows
Every 3 months

Sanitize my sink
Daily

Clean my refrigerator
Monthly

Get a tune up for my car
Every 3 months or based on your car maintenance schedule

9. TRAVEL

It's no secret that millennial women are on the go! As our local and global community becomes more and more connected, many women find themselves traveling frequently for both work and pleasure.

Whether you have never flown on a plane or you're a frequent flyer, traveling can be hectic, overwhelming, and exhausting. In order to ensure that you can make your travel experience as seamless as possible, consider implementing tried and true travel tips that will make your life more efficient and effortless. This chapter will cover:

- Packing Rules for Long or Short Term Travel
- Travel Tips for Millennial Women
- Disruptions in Travel Plans
- Handling a Minor Car Accident
- 5 Ways Save Money When Traveling

Packing Rules for Long or Short Term Travel

The number one rule for comfortable and easy travel is to pack light! With rising costs of travel fees, the frequent occurrence of missing luggage, and the desire to be as efficient as possible when traveling, minimal packing is the key to mastering short or long-term trips.

Effective packing starts with the selection of appropriate luggage. Contrary to popular belief, for most trips shorter than 3 weeks, you can just pack in a carry-on roller and personal item bag. Always be mindful of airline regulations for luggage size and weight. Many carriers have varying domestic and international requirements. If for some reason your luggage is overweight or a non-traditional size, you may spend upwards of $100 in additional fees.

To master packing, consider these tips:

Clothing Selection

- Select clothing and shoes solely based on your trip's itinerary.
- Choose clothing that falls within the same color palate and can be interchanged. Neutral colors such as black, gray, beige, khaki, and white are a great starting point.
- Always pack a basic black cotton dress that can be worn for casual occasions or dressed up with accessories.
- Refrain from packing an outfit for each day. Rather, pack clothing that has multiple purposes and can be washed and re-worn if needed. For example, leggings can be worn with a casual shirt and re-worn under a tunic or skirt.

- Pack light clothing that can be layered or removed as the local temperature changes.

Maximize Your Wardrobe

- Utilize accessories such as scarves, statement necklaces, and other jewelry to enhance and personalize your outfits.
- Pack a limited number of pajamas and use clothing such as lightweight yoga pants or tank tops to serve for both day and sleep wear.
- Minimize your shoes to no more than 3 pairs. Wear your bulkiest shoes on the plane with you. Consider a nice leather sandal or wedge that can transition for casual or dress wear.

Packing Must-Haves

- Bring travel-sized toiletries under 3 oz. or less to reduce headaches when going through security.
- Always bring your own washcloth (or two). Many countries, often in Europe and Africa, do not provide them in hotels.
- Pack clean underwear in your carry-on luggage. This will help for freshening up after a long flight.

Packing Smartly

- Pack your suitcase to take advantage of all spaces and pockets.
- Consider using mesh-packing cubes to help you keep your clothing organized and tidy.
- Use cavities such as the insides of shoes to pack fragile items.

- Always pack extra plastic bags. They can be useful for everything from separating dirty undergarments to keeping jewelry organized.
- Always bring a few packets of laundry detergent in case you need to wash clothing in your room.
- Consider packing a travel compliant air freshener, such as a lavender sachet, in your luggage to keep your belongings fresh. Use the air freshener to keep your hotel accommodations fresh and comfortable.
- Remember that you always need less than you think! If you are debating the necessity of an item, put it back to conserve more space.

Travel Tips for Millennial Women

To ensure an enjoyable and safe experience, consider the following recommendations before your travel and throughout your trip.

Before You Go

- Contact your bank and inform them of your upcoming trip.
- Bring an extra set of inactivated debit cards in case your wallet is stolen, or your card is compromised at an ATM.
- Contact your cellular phone company and inquire about a global data package to reduce surprise fees for roaming and out of area coverage.
- Depending on the length of your trip and destination, visit your doctor to request and fill a prescription for a general antibiotic, yeast/anti-fungal infection medication, and any other pharmaceuticals that may be difficult to obtain.
- Print and carry on copies of your itinerary, flight details, hotel accommodations, and key numbers. Do not rely on your cell phone to keep this information.
- Take a picture and email yourself copies of your important documents (credit cards, passport info, itinerary).
- Obtain global trip and medical insurance. For a nominal cost, trip insurance can provide peace of mind and cover a variety of issues ranging from lost baggage to medical evacuation expenses.
- If using online booking sites that allow you to rent out someone's apartment or home, be sure that the rental has overwhelmingly positive reviews. Seek reviews from other female customers and their perspectives on safety, accessibility to common destinations, and comfort.

- Consider wearing a faux wedding ring
- Research local dress customs
- Pack extra essential feminine products that you may need during your trip. Depending on where you are going, you may be unlikely to find your preferred brand or product.

Getting Settled

- If you are traveling alone, refrain from telling locals you are traveling alone until you are comfortable with your surroundings and have made a few friends.
- Be aware of your surroundings if you are staying in a small hotel or hostel. If for any reason, you do not feel comfortable, consider making different arrangements.
- Finding a trusted taxi driver or chauffeur is invaluable. If you encounter a driver that you trust and who is multilingual, make sure you obtain his or her contact information for trips or emergencies. If you plan on being in the area for a while, consider negotiating a special rate based on frequent usage.
- Make friends with someone who is local who can provide you with insider tips.
- Ask your host of front desk staff to write the name of your hotel/housing on a card. Use this to share with drivers in case there is a language barrier.
- Ask a trusted local to show you how to navigate public transportation. Be sure to ask about potential changes due to weekend schedules.
- If you are traveling alone and with a cab driver, always pretend that you are going to meet a friend when going from destination to destination or sightseeing.
- Refrain from letting a driver or other individual carry your luggage to your room. Do it yourself even if it requires multiple trips.

At All Times

- Watch your alcohol intake and make sure that someone (shop owner, cab driver, doorman, front desk staff, friend) sees that you arrived home safely on late evenings.
- Do not keep all your money in one place.
- Pack light and use a small purse such as a cross body bag when out and about.
- Utilize Wi-Fi in local cafes, hotels, and public spaces for internet browsing and communication.
- Establish a communication plan with loved ones back home. This will help relieve any concern with anxious parents

Disruptions in Travel Plans

Whether you're travelling for work or leisure, you will experience disruptions in your itinerary. Most often, such disturbances or delays will be weather-related and are outside the control of the specific airline company.

Weather-related travel delays can be very frustrating when the sun is shining outside of your terminal window and the cancellation is due to issues within the destination city.

In these circumstances, your airline will announce the delay or cancellation but may refund your ticket or offer a voucher since they have no control over weather patterns. You may feel discouraged, but there is still hope.

1. Approach the ticket counter and obtain the full scoop on the delay and the expected time of the next departure.
2. If the delay is hours long or overnight, ask the ticket agent to look at other airlines for potential flights.
3. If available (and you can afford to do so) book the flight on another airline. Keep in mind, you will not be refunded for abandoning the initial flight unless the airline is liable.
4. If all flights are booked, and you are determined to get to your destination, you can always explore the possibility of a one-way car rental.
5. If you are a frequent traveler, enroll in an airline loyalty membership program, which is often free of charge and gives you points for the frequency of your trips. Based on the level of points, you can reap several benefits, including upgraded travel, free checked luggage, access to airline lounges, and priority boarding.
6. One of the biggest and often under-utilized perks of loyalty membership is the members-only phone help desk. If you find yourself in a travel bind related to delays or

cancellations, 95% of your fellow passengers are going to stand in line waiting to be served by a reservation agent. By being a loyalty member, you can bypass this stress by sitting in your chair, calling the help desk, and letting them do the work for you!

Handling a Minor Car Accident

Being involved in a car accident can be a frightening experience for all the parties. Above all else, you and other passengers' safety should be the top priority.

- Ensure that everyone is ok.
- If the accident is minor, move cars aside.
- Turn off the car engine.
- Stay at the scene and if possible, call the police.
- Locate your driver's license, insurance card, and car registration information.
- Obtain the name, license plate number, and insurance information of the other driver(s). If possible, also obtain their contact information.
- Pull out your camera phone or digital camera and start documenting the scene.
- When the police arrive, give a detailed report.
- Make sure the police officer gives you a report number and instructions on obtaining a copy.
- Call your insurance company and review the details of your auto policy.
- Seek legal and medical attention if necessary and save all receipts generated from damage or other expenses due to the car accident.

5 Ways to Save Money When Traveling

1. Unless you need to be in communication with your work or loved ones in case of an emergency, use free Wi-Fi (hotel or public cafes) for internet surfing and communicating back home.
2. Consider all-inclusive packages when staying at a resort to keep costs transparent and to limit worries about your total bill.
3. If safe, use public transportation for a cost-efficient and scenic way to explore the places you are visiting.
4. If possible, cook for yourself. If your accommodations offer a kitchen, purchase a small amount of groceries at a local store and prepare a few meals at "home." Your wallet and waistline will be thankful.
5. Watch service fees. Prior to traveling abroad, make sure you are aware of banking rules for international service charges and fees.

About the Author

As a professional development expert, author Kelli Clifton Ogunsanya thrives on enabling millennial women to embrace their infinite potential and to lead empowered lives with unshakable confidence and work ethic.

As a trained strategist, public speaker, blog contributor, and executive advisor, Kelli has first-hand experience with the highs and lows of navigating career success across various business sectors. A proud millennial, Kelli balances her professional commitments with community volunteerism, global travel, and entrepreneurism.

Throughout her tenure in corporate America, Kelli has served as a professional development coach to entry to mid-level professionals, millennials, and career changers. With experience as a Big 4 management consultant, Kelli has Fortune 100 client experience leading strategic transformations for healthcare systems, federal agencies, biopharmaceutical companies, and international ministries of health.

Kelli's unique niche is her ability to translate personal and real-time professional experiences into prescriptive guidance and honest conversation. As a debut author, Madame Millennial represents more than 10 years of Kelli's personal experiences in climbing the corporate ladder while aiming to balance work, life, and everything in between.

www.ingramcontent.com/pod-product-compliance
Lightning Source LLC
Chambersburg PA
CBHW021434080526
44588CB00009B/523